TRAY 5

D0107634

The Smithsonian Guides to Natural America
THE SOUTHWEST

MN

WI

MI

The
Great
Lakes

IA

The
Heartland

IL

IN

OH

MO

Central
Appalachia

KY

TN

WV

VA

NY

The
Mid–Atlantic
States

PA

MD DE

Northern
New
England

ME

VT

NH

MA
CT RI

Southern
New
England

The
Atlantic
Coast

NC

SC

The
South
Central
States

AR

MS

LA

AL

The
Southeast

GA

FL

THE SOUTHWEST
ARIZONA – NEW MEXICO

THE SMITHSONIAN GUIDES TO NATURAL AMERICA

THE SOUTHWEST

NEW MEXICO AND ARIZONA

TEXT
Jake Page

PHOTOGRAPHY
George H. H. Huey

PREFACE
Thomas E. Lovejoy

SMITHSONIAN BOOKS • WASHINGTON, D.C.
RANDOM HOUSE • NEW YORK, N.Y.

Copyright © 1995 by Smithsonian Institution
Maps by Allan Cartography. Raven Maps & Images bases are used by permission.
Cover design by Andy Carpenter.
Permission credits to reproduce previously published photos appear on page 286.
All rights reserved under International and Pan-American Copyright Conventions.
Published in the United States by Random House, Inc., New York, and Smithsonian
Books, Washington, D.C., and simultaneously in Canada by Random House of Canada
Limited, Toronto.

Front cover: Shiprock, New Mexico
Half-title page: Monument Valley Tribal Park, Arizona
Frontispiece: Senita Basin, Organ Pipe Cactus National Monument, Arizona
Back cover: mule deer, Arizona; cactus flower; elf owl in saguaro cactus

THE SMITHSONIAN INSTITUTION
SECRETARY I. Michael Heyman
COUNSELOR TO THE SECRETARY FOR
BIODIVERSITY AND ENVIRONMENTAL AFFAIRS Thomas E. Lovejoy
DIRECTOR, SMITHSONIAN PRESS/SMITHSONIAN PRODUCTIONS Daniel H. Goodwin
EDITOR, SMITHSONIAN BOOKS Alexis Doster III

THE SMITHSONIAN GUIDES TO NATURAL AMERICA
SERIES EDITOR Sandra Wilmot
MANAGING EDITOR Ellen Scordato
PHOTO EDITOR Mary Jenkins
ART DIRECTOR Mervyn Clay
ASSISTANT PHOTO EDITOR Ferris Cook
ASSISTANT PHOTO EDITOR Rebecca Williams
ASSISTANT EDITOR Kerry Acker
EDITORIAL ASSISTANT Seth Ginsberg
COPY EDITORS Helen Dunn, Karen Hammonds, Susan Norton
PRODUCTION DIRECTOR Katherine Rosenbloom
DEVELOPMENT EDITOR Mary Luders

Library of Congress Cataloging-in-Publication Data
Page, Jake.
    The Smithsonian guides to natural America. The Southwest—New
Mexico and Arizona/text by Jake Page; photography by George H. H.
Huey.
      p. cm.
    Includes bibliographical references and index.
    ISBN 0-679-76154-3 (pbk.)
    1. Natural history—New Mexico—Guidebooks. 2. Natural history—
Arizona—Guidebooks. 3. New Mexico—Guidebooks. 4. Arizona—
Guidebooks. I. Huey, George H. H. II. Title.
QH105.N6P34 1995   94-33281
508.789—dc20   CIP

Manufactured in the United States of America
98765432

HOW TO USE THIS BOOK

The SMITHSONIAN GUIDES TO NATURAL AMERICA explore and celebrate the preserved and protected natural areas of this country that are open for the public to use and enjoy. From world-famous national parks to tiny local preserves, the places featured in these guides offer a splendid panoply of this nation's natural wonders.

Divided by state and region, this book offers suggested itineraries for travelers, briefly describing the high points of each preserve, refuge, park or wilderness area along the way. Each site was chosen for a specific reason: Some are noted for their botanical, zoological, or geological significance, others simply for their exceptional scenic beauty.

Information pertaining to the area as a whole can be found in the introductory sections to the book and to each chapter. In addition, specialized maps at the beginning of each book and chapter highlight an area's geography and geological features as well as pinpoint the specific locales that the author describes.

For quick reference, places of interest are set in boldface type; those set in boldface followed by the symbol ❖ are listed in the Site Guide at the back of the book. (This feature begins on page 265, just before the index.) Here noteworthy sites are listed alphabetically by state, and each entry provides practical information that visitors need: telephone numbers, mailing addresses, and specific services available.

Addresses and telephone numbers of national, state, and local agencies and organizations are also listed. Also in appendices are a glossary of pertinent scientific terms and designations used to describe natural areas; the author's recommendations for further reading (both nonfiction and fiction); and a list of sources that can aid travelers planning a guided visit.

The words and images of these guides are meant to help both the active naturalist and the armchair traveler to appreciate more fully the environmental diversity and natural splendor of this country. To ensure a successful visit, always contact a site in advance to obtain detailed maps, updated information on hours and fees, and current weather conditions. Many areas maintain a fragile ecological balance. Remember that their continued vitality depends in part on responsible visitors who tread the land lightly.

CONTENTS

PREFACE

ABOVE: *Major John Wesley Powell chats with a Paiute guide during his second Colorado River expedition in 1871.*

Not long ago, accompanied by two of my daughters, I rafted down the Colorado River, surrounded by the awesome geologic history of the Grand Canyon and accompanied by the haunting song of the canyon wren. We hiked out up the Bright Angel Trail—no small feat. Nearing the rim, we felt a strong reluctance to leave the magic spell of this geologic cathedral and reenter the hurly-burly of the modern-day world.

The story of the Colorado River is more than just the story of the Grand Canyon, one of the grandest spectacles in all of natural America. It is also the saga of one-armed John Wesley Powell and his first descent of the river and its mighty rapids in wooden boats. It is also the story of Powell's prescient vision of the constraints imposed by the arid lands west of the 100th Meridian as Americans surged westward. It is a story still relevant today, as the West struggles with the very issues of development and scarce water foreseen by Powell, a giant of an American scientist who at one point worked in the Smithsonian Castle and who had so much to do with the creation of the United States Geological Survey in 1879.

However, the nature of Arizona is more than just geological, the fascinating rocky formations of the Grand Canyon, the Painted

PRECEDING PAGES: *Yellow brittlebrush lights up Arizona's Grass Canyon; incense from its fragrant resin once perfumed mission churches.*

Desert, Meteor Crater, and the Petrified Desert notwithstanding. Here, after a rain, the desert bursts into magnificent, if prickly, blooms, so varied and so vividly beautiful that in a world where most magazines come and go, *Arizona Highways*, which enthralled me as a youth, continues to thrive on this biological kaleidoscope.

In Arizona and New Mexico, one can see more distinctly than anywhere else in natural America the changes in plant and animal communities that appear as one goes up in altitude. The higher peaks are isolated, relatively cool "sky islands," each with its individual assemblage, separated from other such "islands" by the high temperatures of the intervening desert floor. Pioneering biologist C. Hart Merriam (1855–1942), encouraged in his endeavors by Smithsonian Secretary Spencer Baird, conducted some of the definitive work on these altitude-defined life zones on the ranch of the Babbitt family, early settlers in Arizona.

In a seemingly predestined intertwining of institutions and people, Merriam became the first director of the United States Biological Survey. Today, the last remnants of that agency are embodied in the persons of Interior Department scientists who actually work in the Smithsonian's Museum of Natural History. In 1993, they became employees of the new National Biological Survey, created by Secretary of the Interior and former Arizona governor Bruce Babbitt, in a reorganization in which I was honored to be involved.

The Southwest is also that part of America where the presence of the original inhabitants, both past and present, is most marked. The evidence of the mysterious Anasazi people, for example, is pervasive, reaching spectacular and commanding prominence in Arizona's Canyon de Chelly. The oldest fully authenticated human artifacts in the Western Hemisphere were found in New Mexico, near the towns of Clovis and Folsom. Literally everywhere here, one can encounter American Indians and their current cultures, still close to and sensitive to natural America.

OVERLEAF: *First published in 1882, this fine panorama of the Grand Canyon from Point Sublime was created by artist-topographer William H. Holmes.*

New Mexico, more a state of plains than of mountains, is evocative of yet another significant strand of American history, that of Spanish America. Santa Fe, New Mexico, was the capital of one of the four viceroyalties of colonial Spanish America. Just translating Spanish names yields a sense of the richness of our Spanish-American experience. Remarkable in itself, this heritage has also influenced American culture in fundamental, often unnoticed ways. A radiant depiction of the Virgin of Saint Carmel by a New Mexico religious group called the Penitentes inspired the Disney version of Snow White.

The Southwest's combination of dramatic nature and rich culture has been a magnet for creative Americans. It should not surprise us that Georgia O'Keeffe, Frank Lloyd Wright, and flocks of others— poets, philosophers, and scientists—have been drawn to the region.

The author of this volume is an old friend, although I haven't seen him for a long time. A few years ago, Jake Page was seduced by the Southwest, and was transformed into a literal and literate desert rat. Like that estimable creature, he has become intricately adapted to the extreme conditions of his environment.

Thus you could not have a better guide to introduce you to this special region of natural America. Give it half a chance, and you will understand why it approaches sacrilege that the average visitor to the Grand Canyon spends but 15 minutes in the chasm itself. But you don't need to visit the "ultimate" to appreciate the magnificent nature of these two states. Here, almost every road is a scenic highway, and the skies, the sunsets, and the stars are to celebrate. Just realize that, once you go, you may, like Jake, fall permanently under the Southwest's spell.

—Thomas E. Lovejoy

Counselor to the Secretary for
Biodiversity and Environmental Affairs,
SMITHSONIAN INSTITUTION

LEFT: *Wild mint flourishes on the summit of McNight Mountain, the highest point of the Black Range in New Mexico's Aldo Leopold Wilderness Area.*

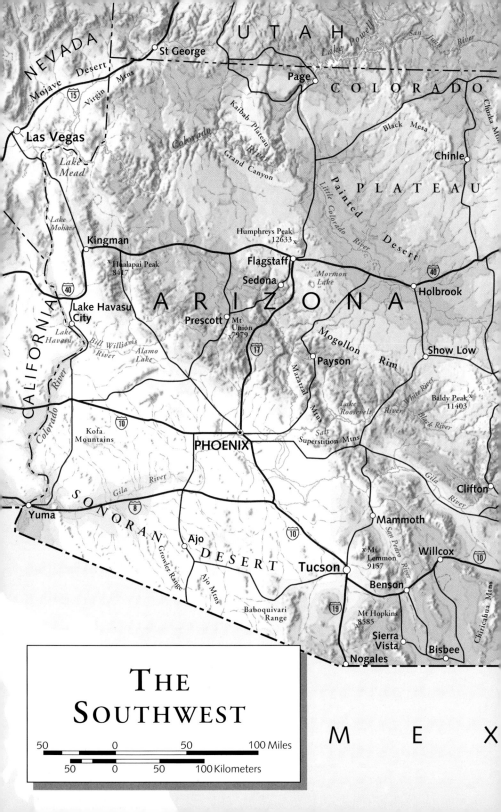

INTRODUCTION
THE SOUTHWEST

In 1863, Abraham Lincoln signed the bill that separated the territory of New Mexico into two entities, New Mexico and Arizona. At the time, people of northern European heritage had only recently begun to seek a living in Arizona north of Tucson, and the inhabitants of that sleepy town had only recently become Americans (by virtue of the 1853 Gadsden Purchase). A straight line was drawn south to north, miraculously meeting the similar line that separates Utah and Colorado and making that infinitely tiny point the only one in the United States shared by four states. A surveyor's marvel, the Four Corners region has little to do with the nature of the two states south of it. Such lines on maps are of little import to biologists and geologists, or to the vast slow-motion upheavals that have shaped the land, and the infinitely creative efforts of life to sustain itself there. Those timeless forces overlap, merge, in disregard of maps. Nevertheless, in this book the two states are treated separately as a matter of convenience.

The border between these two states and the republic of Mexico seems, on the other hand, to coincide roughly with some significant natural distinctions. Only in certain favorable pockets of southern New Mexico and Arizona can one see a few dozen Mexican species of birds, for example, and to these pockets birders come from far and wide to forward their life lists. The same is true of many other creatures from rodents to trees, although rodent- and tree-watchers are less common than bird-watchers.

There *are* historic distinctions between the two states. Spanish conquistadores began pushing north up the Rio Grande into this realm well before Jamestown and Plymouth received the British in the early 1600s. By the time of Miles Standish, the Spaniards and the mestizos (persons of mixed Indian and Spanish ancestry) who accompanied

---

PRECEDING PAGES: *Early sunlight glances from the ragged Kofa Mountains in western Arizona's Kofa National Wildlife Refuge and will soon burn down on cactus, ocotillo, and other hardy desert dwellers.*

them had established a capital well up the Rio Grande near San Juan Pueblo. They later moved it south to Santa Fe, which today is the oldest capital in the nation (counting its territorial status as the political center of Nueva Mexico). This ancient Spanish influence remains considerable in the state of New Mexico: Descendants of the conquistadores are still anchored in their northern strongholds in the high country, and many others conduct their daily business throughout the state. On the other hand, the Spanish did not progress very far into today's Arizona because they ran into the Apache.

The era before the Spanish is all called prehistory because we are unable to read the hundreds of thousands of written records left pecked in stone. This prehistory extends back into an unimaginable past, marked in virtually every potentially salubrious place by old ruins, both simple and sophisticated. But more important, the past is recalled by present-day descendants of those ancient people. In many cases, the multifarious and polyglot tribes of the Colorado River and the Rio Grande—the Hopi, Navajo, Hualapai, Pima, Papago, and Apache—live in the same places they have always lived. Much of the two states remains Indian country (and the term Indian is politically correct locally), home to nearly a fifth of all American Indians. The rest of us, having followed the Indians and the Hispanics, are latecomers, often lumped together as Anglos (another inaccurate convenience). This region proudly boasts of its three cultures and in fact contains countless cultures within cultures. In New Mexico and Arizona, these define and lend earthy and primary color to the social tapestry that no visitor fails to sense. Many first-timers to the area feel they have entered a foreign country. Particularly in New Mexico, some wonder if they have crossed a border not shown on their roadmaps. The same feeling prevails in the great tristate expanses of the Navajo Reservation, or the nearly medieval ambience of the Hopi villages in northeastern Arizona, or in the polyglot city of Tucson. In these two states, one simply cannot avoid the realization that we inhabit only a fraction of the mysterious continuum of civilization in this ancient place. In this sentiment, the land colludes.

OVERLEAF: *Artist Thomas Moran made the Grand Canyon part of the national consciousness with such majestic pictures as* **Chasm of the Colorado,** *painted in 1873, which hung in the U.S. Capitol until the 1930s.*

Desert is what many correctly envision in New Mexico and Arizona. And the desert suggests a kind of timelessness in its ancient cacti—40-foot saguaro sentinels standing in the hot, changeless dust or a sea of prickly cholla cacti tearing at the chaps of passing *vaqueros* (cowboys). Four different types of desert exist in these two states, one in New Mexico and all four in Arizona.

In New Mexico, the Chihuahuan Desert thrusts two arms halfway up the state from the Mexican area for which it is named. Here, as in deserts everywhere, altitude is a key factor. While the land ranges from 1,000 feet along the Rio Grande to 6,500 feet in Mexico, for the most part the altitude lies between 3,500 and 5,000 feet. At such elevations, the winters are relatively cold and long (with up to a hundred nights of freezing temperatures), but the summers are extremely hot, with many days in the hundreds. It rains in the Chihuahuan Desert—about eight to twelve inches a year—and most of this precipitation comes from short thunderstorms during the summer. The moderately high rainfall and intermittently cool temperatures combine with calcium-rich soils to make a special environment for desert vegetation. Numerous plants thrive, primarily creosote bush, grasses, yuccas, and agaves (or century plants), along with a host of cacti such as prickly pears and chollas.

From southern New Mexico, the Chihuahuan Desert extends across the border into Arizona, where most of the desertlands are Sonoran. A young desert, the Sonoran has existed in its present form for only 10,000 years. It survives on a highly varied geological platform where mountains have heaved up, great blocks of land have collapsed, and volcanoes have erupted. All this activity has created a diverse habitat in the lowlands or basins, usually 3,000 feet or less in elevation, where the Sonoran Desert occurs. The plants have responded in kind: The Sonoran is the most botanically diverse of the North American deserts. Not only are there more kinds of plants, but they also take on different forms. Such diversity appears because the Sonoran is a subtropical desert,

RIGHT: *Brittlebrush makes a yellow carpet around a lone saguaro cactus in Lost Dutchman State Park, which lies in the lee of the Superstition Mountains, the northern limit of Arizona's Sonoran Desert.*

ABOVE: *Barren and unforgiving, but a holy realm nonetheless, the Adeiiechii cliffs command the horizon near Cameron in Navajoland, a*

generally lower in altitude than the Chihuahuan. Thanks to the peculiar effects of the California mountains, this desert receives both summer and winter rains, which promotes a different kind of vegetation.

In the United States, the most characteristic Sonoran species is the stately saguaro cactus, but many other cacti occur—barrel, teddybear, fishhook, hedgehog, and a variety of chollas. Creosote bush is common (although more densely leaved than in the Chihuahuan Desert), as is the ocotillo, a tall plant made up of numerous long stems. A saguaro relative, the organ-pipe cactus, grows in parts of the Sonoran as well. Indeed, the plant list is so long that the Sonoran is often called the "Green Desert."

The Mojave Desert, ranging mostly in California, reaches over into the central and northern portions of Arizona. This desert is characterized by distantly spaced shrubs, the treelike yucca called the Joshua tree, severely high temperatures, and a little bit of rain in winter that creates a great

reservation that comprises most of northeastern Arizona and part of New Mexico and Utah and surrounds the smaller realm of the Hopi.

bloom of color in early spring—the heyday of the ephemerals, those evanescent plants that often flower for only a few days. Flowers, frogs, cacti, and most of the other plants must react very quickly to the sporadic arrival of moisture because it will be followed, usually, by a long drought. It is said that W. C. Fields, while out on a walk at a Mojave Desert spa, spotted a magnificent wildflower. The next day he asked a friend to visit it with him and found to his amazement that it was not there. Enraged, he thrashed the innocent plant with his stick, shouting, "Bloom, damn you, bloom!"

The fourth desert type in Arizona—occurring only in the extreme northwestern corner—is the Great Basin Desert. The largest of the four types, it extends up into Oregon. Overall, it supports fewer species of plants, and most cacti are missing. Appearing at high elevations, 4,000 feet and above, it is dominated by sagebrush and saltbush (also common

in the Sonoran and Chihuahuan deserts). On the drier parts of the Colorado Plateau a sagebrush-grassland mix occurs, which ecologists do not classify as a desert even though it exhibits many of the characteristics of the Great Basin Desert (notably, a lot of sagebrush). In many parts of New Mexico and Arizona, overgrazing of what was essentially grassland has enabled sagebrush to take over. It happily pioneers in such disturbed land and can choke out the native grasses: Thus man is extending a version of the Great Basin Desert into places where it never existed.

The deserts of Arizona and New Mexico, almost all of them dry, sunblasted basins between jagged mountain ranges, are some of the region's most spectacular and haunting natural places. From the too-brilliantly white sands of White Sands National Monument to the deathly stillness of the Painted Desert, they are the kinds of places that a nineteenth-century trekker, John Van Dyke, had in mind when he wrote, "Who shall paint the splendor of [the desert's] light; and from the rising up of the sun to the going down of the moon over the iron mountains, the glory of its wondrous coloring!"

ABOVE: *The state bird of New Mexico and a relative of the cuckoo, the often-seen roadrunner is a versatile and oddly comical desert predator that feeds chiefly on lizards, scorpions, and a variety of insects.*

LEFT: *Common in open, brushy areas, the black-tailed jack (a hare) can achieve a speed of up to 40 miles per hour in spurts, but relays of coyotes can wear it out. Both roadrunner and hare do quite well in areas of relatively dense human habitation, as does the highly adaptive coyote.*

M any visitors are surprised to find landscapes other than deserts in Arizona and New Mexico. But the Rocky Mountains end in New Mexico, as do the Great Plains. Whole landscapes are virtually the sole creation of ancient and recent volcanoes. The second greatest rift valley in the world occurs here, as does the greatest canyon on the planet.

There are thousands of lesser

13

canyons—lesser in scope and grandeur, perhaps, but each containing its own secrets. There are more than two hundred separate mountain ranges—some jumbled and thickly forested and others lined up like compass needles—as well as mountain streams and lakes. There are great caverns full of nature's oddest sculpture, and thousands of caves, windblown out of vermilion and yellow and purple cliffs. There are the mesas and gorges of the Colorado Plateau, a vast, unified plate of high country (the second largest such feature in the world); its southern edge, the Mogollon Rim (pronounced "Mogey-on" and named for an early governor of Nueva Mexico), drops off 2,000 feet in places. Indeed, these two states harbor an unparalleled diversity of landforms—and life-forms. More than half the bird species known in North America can be seen in a single county.

It is odd that the key to understanding the astonishing variety of a land often envisioned as mostly flat is elevation. In the 1880s, the naturalist C. Hart Merriam, by virtue of his federally sponsored explorations of the West, particularly northern Arizona, devised a theory of distinct life zones based on temperature. And temperature is, in such places, largely a function of elevation. Essentially, as one proceeds from the desert floor up to the highest peak, one passes through several fairly distinct belts of vegetation—as though one traveled from the Mexican border to Hudson's Bay in Canada. From sea level to about 4,500 feet, the desert plants discussed above predominate; this area is often called the Lower Sonoran zone.

From 4,500 to 6,500 feet, the dominant plant community is pinyon pine, Utah juniper, and other species such as saltbush and greasewood, often interspersed among grama grassland. The dark pines and junipers make the land look, as D. H. Lawrence pointed out, as though it were covered with leopard's spots. Sagebrush is also common at this altitude, sometimes taking over altogether. As in any zone, the boundaries may be ragged: Cacti and yuccas may creep into this Upper Sonoran zone. Streamside, or riparian, plants are dominated by cottonwoods, walnuts, and sycamores, and in drier areas shrubs such as Apache plume, fernbush, and scrub oak are found. Typically, the trees do not achieve much height, and these pinyon-juniper woodlands are often called pygmy forests.

Above, from 6,500 to 8,000 feet, is the Transition zone, a belt of mostly pines and oaks, often salted with silver and blue spruces. Ponderosa pines and Gambel oaks are dominant. The trees, particularly the tall ponderosas, typically grow in open parklike stands, though on cooler northern slopes the ponderosa stands tend to be thicker and may share the slope with Douglas firs from the zone above. Shrubs and trees from the Upper Sonoran zone, such as sage, mountain mahogany, and box elder, reach their highest elevation just inside this zone. Here also are hawthorns, roses, and in the south, Arizona cypresses, along with Arizona, Chihuahua, and Apache pines.

From 8,000 to 9,500 feet, the forest changes greatly in aspect, thanks to the typically 25 to 30 inches of annual precipitation—twice that of the pinyon-juniper forests below. Here the trees—Douglas firs and white-trunked aspens—grow more densely, and the sun rarely hits the forest floor. Common juniper and white fir also occur, along with lodgepole pine, a pioneer species that moves in after a fire, as does aspen. On slopes with a southern exposure, ponderosas creep upward; these areas are often considered part of the Transition zone.

From 9,500 to 11,500 feet, the dominant trees are Engelmann spruces and subalpine firs, along with blue spruces and (in the south) Mexican white pines. After a fire, lodgepole pines move in here as well. Annual precipitation ranges from 30 to 90 inches, much of it snow, which remains well into the spring. In the upper reaches of this Hudsonian, or subalpine, zone, the strong winds and poor soils sustain only stunted and dwarfed members of these species. At tree line, among the stunted subalpine varieties, are found those longest-living of trees, bristlecone pines.

Above 11,500 feet is the windswept Arctic or Alpine zone, where there is little more than low scrub and a few grasses and hardy flowering plants. This zone is found on only a handful of mountaintops in New Mexico and Arizona.

Each zone is home to characteristic animals as well. Spotted skunks, ringtails, pocket mice, jackrabbits, various lizards, and other common desert creatures live in the Lower Sonoran, along with pronghorns. Gray foxes and mule deer appear with various rock squirrels and chipmunks. Above, among the ponderosas, Abert's squirrels, porcupines, and mule

OVERLEAF: *Presiding above grasslands reminiscent of those of Pleistocene times, the Animas range of southern New Mexico's bootheel stretches north from near the summit of Animas Peak.*

deer emerge. In the Hudsonian zone, red squirrels are commonly seen. And in these less trammeled upper regions of the mountains are black bears, mountain lions, and bobcats (rarely seen in the flesh, but their signs are often noted), as well as elk and, in a few regions, bighorn sheep.

In all, the two states cover some 150 million acres, of which about 60 million are held by such agencies as the United States Forest Service, the Bureau of Land Management, the National Park Service, and the military. The reservations of 48 American Indian tribes occupy more than 30 million acres. Slightly more than 5 million people live in the two states, averaging 20 persons per square mile, but the vast majority reside in a handful of metropolitan areas—Phoenix, Tucson, Albuquerque. Enormous tracts of federal land, along with state and local parks, are available for outdoor recreation, and pressure on those lands—especially the ones near major metropolitan areas—continues to grow. The two states face a mounting number of very complex environmental problems. This book is no place to examine these matters in detail, but a few words about some basic principles are in order.

To begin with, in a land classified as largely semiarid to desert, most of the environmental problems center directly on, or indirectly involve, water. An anthropologist once tape-recorded a Hopi Indian who had agreed to sing the most important Hopi songs for him. The anthropologist duly recorded them, had them translated, and then complained that they were all about water. The old Hopi nodded, explaining that the Hopi sing only for what they lack. (He went on to point out that all the white man's songs seem to be about love.)

There are two basic attitudes in the Southwest about water—both called "conservation" by their adherents. People of European descent opened up the West as a place to be exploited, to be lived in, and to be rearranged wherever possible. Conservation of water meant that none was wasted. A river's water was put to work, not left to run uselessly out to sea. To old-line westerners—particularly ranchers, miners, and farmers—conservation means use. National forests are tree farms—which was their original purpose and explains why the National Forest Service is part of the United States Department of Agriculture—and places to herd cattle by permit. One cannot "use" a vista.

To environmentalists in the tradition of naturalist Rachel Carson, con-

ABOVE: *Hovering in midair, a broad-tailed hummingbird, one of three hummers common throughout much of Arizona and New Mexico, prepares to make the most of a tempting scarlet penstemon array.*

servation means an almost entirely different thing—limited use of resources with emphasis on the ethical as well as aesthetic value of wildness. To them, national forests are far more than merely practical resources; they are places dedicated to public enjoyment (which is not enhanced by cattle upstream or the vista of a clearcut woodland).

Both kinds of conservationists exist in the Southwest, and most of the area's environmental problems will be settled only by an accommodation of the two interpretations or by the disappearance of one side. Each view has its indisputable merits—and many disputable ones. About the only Southwestern environmental problem likely to affect readers of this book is overuse by recreationists. The land is a place of beauty to be enjoyed on foot, on horseback, or from an automobile. In these pages, we mention some places that are happily thronged by the millions, some places that show varying degrees of wear and tear, and some that are relatively untrammeled. We have attempted to highlight the natural places where one may experience the region's astonishing diversity and endless beauty, amid crowds or in solitude. We hope that those who travel to

The Southwest

RIGHT: *Little has changed since 1904 when Edward Curtis photographed Navajo horsemen passing by the towering sandstone walls of Canyon de Chelly, a traditional Navajo stronghold and sacred place.*

these places will tread lightly, take nothing from them, and leave nothing behind but footprints. We also hope that visitors will find here natural places that especially resonate and return to them, perhaps even take up their cause.

An aspect of the Southwest that immediately confronts visitors to its natural places is that much of the land remains Indian country. Although Indian reservations are under the stewardship of the federal government, the tribes are largely sovereign in law and in the ways they officially or unofficially receive visitors. Several tribes—notably, the Navajo in the north and the Apache in the south—actively promote tourism on their reservations (camping, fishing, sightseeing) and have designated such areas in the form of campgrounds and tribal parks. A number of those places are noted in this book. Some of Indian country's most attractive features, however, and a few in this book, are not so designated, and in those areas visitors should seek out a tribal guide by applying at the tribe's headquarters or by asking someone at a nearby trading post or reservation motel.

Typically, Indians do not own land outright as private property; they live on it, farm it, or run sheep on it as part of a traditional family or clan arrangement that goes back generations if not eons. Visitors, however, are best advised to consider all tribal lands private property and not enter them without permission.

These Indian lands are populated in another way. For most Indian res-

idents, the land is enriched by the very real presence of spirits, what the
Navajo call Holy People, the immortal essences of such things as rocks,
thunder, squirrels, ants. The land is filled as well with unmarked
shrines—holy places that exist within the overall holiness of Mother
Earth herself. Indians tend to speak in soft voices, in part so as not to
interfere with the Holy People with whom they share the land. This at-
titude is alien to many non-Indian visitors and residents in the Southwest, but when on Indian lands they are advised to respect it, if not actively adopt it, by understanding that they are in the equivalent of a
church. Indeed, visitors can enhance their experience of the natural
places in this book if they try to imagine them in such a manner, because all of them were once Indian country.

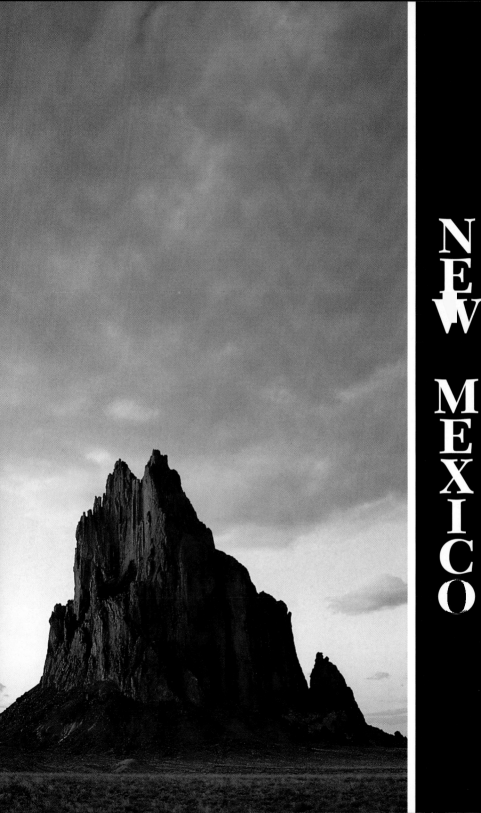

NEW MEXICO

PART ONE

NEW MEXICO

The most important natural area in New Mexico exists wherever one goes in the state. It is the sky overhead. For overhead is the great light show, the special quality people find in New Mexico that they cannot quite describe (the English language, perhaps the richest in the world in numbers of words, lacks fine distinctions about matters that are both meteorological and aesthetic). The sky and its sun are, in New Mexico, the soul-catchers. In one place in fifteen minutes, the sky may change from an overall gray that produces a few snowflakes, to a blue deeper than any ocean with breathlessly light clouds almost hurtling across it, to an opaque yellow as the spring winds hit, shifting enormous quantities of Arizona "topsoil" eastward.

In New Mexico, on a proper day, every leaf of every creosote bush, every lavender wild-aster petal, every sunstruck rock face on a mountain miles off, stands out with a clarity that is existential. In such a light, the importance of a single rock, an individual flower, the existence of life itself, can strike one suddenly—fresh and poignant. What is distant seems near; what is near seems searingly real, insistent, poised. And with each change in the arc of the sun, especially at the beginning and end of its daily career, and with each passing cloud when they are present, the entire stage setting for the Creation is new, something never seen before.

The Sandia Mountains, for example, which lie like a blessed guard dog in silent enormity to the east of New Mexico's largest city, Albuquerque, are named for the color of the inside of a watermelon. Given the right configuration of things in the evening sky, the

---

PRECEDING PAGES: *Shiprock soars 1,100 feet from the surrounding desert. The Navajo's sacred "Rock with Wings" is an ancient volcanic remnant.*

24

mountains glow as if from within, and the name makes sense. But the Sandias change color, mood, and even shape many times in every hour of daylight. They are the playmates of the sun, which, even as it dips behind the western horizon with nothing but high clouds to turn gold and copper and apricot and vermilion, doesn't want to relinquish its place—doesn't want to go to bed. The glow remains, an amber cloud presides over a gunmetal-gray veil of distant rain, and distant canyons emit countershafts of pale light.

At such moments, a visible hymn is in the air, sung with an elegiac purity.

Every vista in the state, every landform and ecosystem, whether it is unimaginable miles away or within the intimate confines of an adobe wall, is a creature of New Mexico's elusive, even angelic light.

The English novelist of the twenties D. H. Lawrence saw it somewhat differently. In fact, he grew quite terrified of the New Mexico landscape. He wrote: "The first moment I saw the brilliant, proud morning shine high up over the deserts of Santa Fe, something stood still in my soul, and I started to attend. . . . Never is the light more pure and overweening than there, arching with a royalty almost cruel over the hollow, uptilted world."

Few have looked for the first time upon the many landscapes of New Mexico without feeling an upwelling of emotion, a sense of their own size. "Rising out of long forgotten seas like a massive shrug of shoulders," wrote John Dewitt McKee, a professor of English, in the 1950s, "the mountains stand firm and hold us. Volcanic cones against the sky, monuments to the grandeur of past violence, hold us too, in something that approaches awe." And then come the aftereffects. McKee said: "The land itself by slow degrees takes those who come to it and shapes them till they fit, till they take the color of the desert, till they can look almost unwaveringly at the sky. This is the land then."

And so it remains today, under its uptilted world of sky and light.

OVERLEAF: *In the undulating and intensely colored* Rust Red Hills *(1930), Georgia O'Keeffe distills the essence of the New Mexico landscape.*

ACROSS THE TOP: NORTHERN NEW MEXICO

United States Route 64 starts in Nags Head, North Carolina, and ends in a tiny Navajo settlement, Teec Nos Pos, just across the border from New Mexico in Arizona. The last 400 miles cross the northern reaches of New Mexico, some of the most beautiful and varied country in the nation and typical of the surprising variety of southwestern landscapes. Entering the state from Oklahoma, Route 64 crosses the rolling grasslands of the western end of the Great Plains and rises slightly into a land littered with the immense remnants, some quite recent, of volcanic violence. Cones and lava flows, some old enough to be well worn and dusted with scrubby trees, rise in a fine chaotic profusion from flat land.

From Raton to Cimarron, Route 64 follows the path of the Santa Fe Trail, where along the road one can still glimpse the old wagon ruts of the early commerce that brought a rough, roiling Anglo presence into the relatively timeless Spanish world of early nineteenth-century New Mexico. Leaving the last of the plains country, the highway rises through the 600-foot granite cliffs of Cimarron Canyon into the southern Rocky Mountains, thickly forested with pine, fir, and spruce, through breathtaking high-country valleys and past the state's tallest

LEFT: *Greasewood and saltbush beckon visitors toward the eerie and silent realm of the Bisti Badlands, an area of eroded clay beds, caprock, and the occasional black stripe bespeaking a coal seam.*

mountain, Wheeler Peak, to Taos, the old Indian pueblo, art colony, and increasingly busy tourist and ski center.

From there, on the second-highest suspension bridge in the country, the highway crosses the Rio Grande Gorge and climbs back up into the Rocky Mountains and through the old Spanish settlements in the Chama Valley, places with names like Tierra Amarilla and Los Ojos, still seats of old Spanish ways. The route rises again into the mountainous lands of the Jicarilla Apache, the reservation of a northern group of this once wide-ranging tribe of nomadic Indians. Here, as elsewhere in the mountains, elk, mule deer, bobcats, and mountain lions roam free, and mountain lakes teem with fish. The route descends through hills and canyons to the Colorado Plateau, where it meets the San Juan River. Nearby, a dam has created the largest body of water in northern New Mexico, Navajo Lake, a lodestar for campers and (particularly below the dam) fishermen.

Soon the route cuts through oil and gas country, a seemingly long and heavily built-up strip from Bloomfield through Farmington and past the Four Corners Power Plant, a vast coal-fired engine of civilization that holds out at least one surprise for the naturalist. Here and beyond is a land of naked rock and mesas stretching north to the San Juan Mountains, looming like white teeth on the northern horizon. To the south are long stretches of low, dry land, some of it out-and-out badlands, the two landscapes separated by the green arrow of riparian and agricultural land of the San Juan River. Beyond lies the soaring monument called Shiprock, symbol of the Navajo Nation, which stretches from this point west almost to Flagstaff, Arizona.

Far to the south of Shiprock, flanked to the west by the towering Chuska Mountains, the road (no longer Route 64) leads to other mountains, other badlands, a vast region that still echoes with ancient and continuing legend.

THE PLAINS: EAST TO WEST

Just across the border from Oklahoma and for 11 miles to the town of Clayton, the world spreads out north and south of Route 64 in vast treeless plains of thick, lush, surprising grass. This is one of two sections of the **Kiowa National Grasslands❖,** a testament to the restorability (to a nearly natural state) of the overgrazed, overworked land so common

NORTHERN NEW MEXICO

25 Miles

25 Kilometers

0

0

25

25

25

ABOVE: *A dramatic midday squall hovers over the Kiowa National Grasslands in eastern New Mexico, where ranchers and foresters combined to restore the original plant life of the short-grass prairie.*

throughout the entire Great Plains. Like most of eastern New Mexico, this grassy prairie was part of the Dust Bowl of the 1930s, a windblown and sandblasted realm of failed farms. In the late 1930s, the federal government bought up the farms in an area of 25,000 square miles (and another larger area southeast of Springer), reseeded the land, and let it rest. As part of the U.S. Forest Service's national grasslands, the land was intended to provide good grazing to livestock owners.

Grass grew, as it will, but not richly enough to make grazing by permit profitable. In the 1980s, the Forest Service began a radical, counterintuitive experiment based on the theories of a Rhodesian range-management consultant, Allan Savory. Previously, these rangelands had supported great herds of bison, elk, and pronghorns—and had thrived.

For protection against wolves and coyotes, the herds stayed closely bunched, grazing intensely in one area, then quickly moving on. In the process they trampled some grass into the soil, mulching it, and gouged out open places for new grass to grow. The grasses then regrew more densely. On the other hand, without predators, cattle tended to drift around slowly, widely spread out.

To simulate the high concentrations of the old days, with grazing herds constantly on the move, the grasslands were fenced into paddocks where ranchers keep large numbers of cattle for short periods, then move them into other paddocks. On average it takes about 50 days for the grass to regrow—and proliferate. Blue grama and buffalo grasses thrive. Western wheatgrass emerges in the valleys, needle grass on the higher ground. Wildflowers that have not been seen for generations carpet the land if the spring season is wet. And here and there sand bluestem grass shows up, a "climax species" that bespeaks the prairies of the old days.

Pronghorns, nearly extinct here a hundred years ago, are now on the increase; small herds of them, sharing the protein with cattle, can occasionally be seen from the road. This is one of the few places where cows and nature are not at odds—an experiment that could have profound implications for many overgrazed parts of the United States.

Most visitors simply drive through these lands, but the Forest Service office in Clayton provides information for those who want to hike out into the grass.

The Kiowa grasslands lie above the sand and gravel beds of the Ogallala Aquifer, a vast underground region permeated with water; at Clayton, up on an old lava flow surface, the influence of old and not so old volcanoes begins. Twelve miles north of Clayton on Route 370 is **Clayton Lake State Park❖,** a 440-acre wildlife preserve where a lake, created by damming Seneca Creek, provides a seasonal home for various grebes, ducks, and other waterfowl. Migrating sandhill cranes sometimes stop off here in October and late February. In a two-acre exposure of old sandstone, one can see more than 500 dinosaur footprints.

Some 50 miles northwest of Clayton along Route 64 is **Capulin Volcano National Monument❖.** Here one of the most recent cinder

cones in the United States rises in nearly perfect symmetry a thousand feet above the plain. About twelve miles northwest of Capulin Volcano is the Folsom Man site, where excavations in 1928 revealed distinctive artifacts along with the remains of a long-extinct species of giant bison. Indeed, people in the neighborhood probably fled in terror when the volcano blew its stack sometime between 8000 and 2500 B.C., one of the most recent eruptions in the area.

Accidents of nature served the cone well. It consists almost entirely of volcanic cinders thrown up in the initial eruption as pebble-sized bits of light volcanic material: Some fused into rock on contact, others remained loose and unfused. Capulin retained its shapeliness because the lava flows that followed did not spill out of the crater and deform it. Instead, at the bottom of the western slope, dark lava repeatedly escaped from a boca (mouth), some in lumps, some in fluid streams. And before long, the cone was protected from erosion by a good growth of pinyon pine, juniper, mountain mahogany, and other plants including chokecherry (*capulin* in Spanish).

From the visitor center, a road leads up the cone to a parking lot, the trailhead for a .2-mile hike down into the crater and the Crater Rim Trail (1 mile), which circles the crater. Every summer, on the east side of this trail, vast swarms of ladybugs that have overwintered in the high country emerge and bedeck the trees, thence to seek aphids in the lands below. From the rim, a magnificent, tortured land stretches away for miles. In all, some 100 volcanoes helped to produce this region's landscape, a flat plain dotted with eroded volcanic mountains, lava-capped hills, small cinder cones, and mesas topped by horizontal lava flows. On the skyline to the north are the oldest volcanic rocks of the region—the Mesa de Maya on the Colorado border—and to the southeast is Sierra Grande, the largest free-standing mountain in the United States and, at 8,720 feet elevation, the highest point in the United States between longitude 104 and the Atlantic Ocean. Sierra Grande was the product of lava flows, not cinders, and is thus less steep than the curvaceous Capulin.

A detour south on Route 455, then west on Route 505, leads to

LEFT: *A deep pink wild rose and a prickly pear cactus with a frilly, startlingly golden blossom are among the wildflowers that thrive— along with cattle and wildlife—in the Kiowa National Grasslands.*

Maxwell National Wildlife Refuge❖, where three lakes and associated wetlands provide some of the best birding in northeastern New Mexico. Established for migrating waterfowl, it is also an excellent place for raptors, including, in the winter, bald and golden eagles. In all, more than two hundred species have been recorded.

Between Cimarron and Eagle Nest, the plains are left behind. On either side of Route 64, numerous campsites compose **Cimarron Canyon State Park❖,** providing a popular way of enjoying the rugged, narrow gorge cut into the mountains by the Cimarron River. Stretching north and south from the canyon and the highway is the 33,000-acre **Colin Neblett Wildlife Area❖.** The largest wildlife area in New Mexico, it is frequented in season by hunters, often on horseback, on the track of elk, bears, mountain lions, and deer. This is rugged, heavily forested land, with several little-used trails for hiking into the backcountry. Four miles north of Eagle Nest on Route 38 are the ruins of a former mining community, Elizabethtown, and the old dumps provide good hunting for rhodochrosite, fluorite, galena, and other minerals. Due west looms Wheeler Peak, at 13,161 feet the highest mountain in New Mexico and Arizona, beckoning one into the Rocky Mountains.

THE ROCKIES

Split in two by the Rio Grande valley, the Rocky Mountains reach their southern end in New Mexico, the Tusas and Brazos ranges to the west, and in the east reaching as far south as Santa Fe, the Sangre de Cristo Range ("Blood of Christ," so named in the last century by a local offshoot of the Roman Catholic Church, the Penitentes). These mountains are for the most part richly cloaked with forests, giving birth to cold streams, and dotted with shimmering mountain lakes and aspen-fringed meadows. The northern mountains, in the **Carson National Forest❖,** include some of the state's finest high country. One of the most popular hiking places in the forest is the **Wheeler Peak Wilderness,** a 20,000-acre area that is accessible from several directions, including a trail that

---

RIGHT: *Morning greets one of the largest volcanic cinder cones in the world, Capulin Volcano; its eruption sent prehistoric locals (known from fossils as Folsom Man) scurrying for their lives.*

ABOVE: *A rabbit relative often seen peering from talus slopes of alpine areas and spruce-fir forests, a pika near the timberline gathers food that it will cure in the sun and later store for winter provisions.*

originates in the upper parking area at the Taos Ski Valley. The shortest way to the top is a four-mile hike to Williams Lake, nestled among craggy peaks in a glacial basin on the western base of Wheeler Peak, and then a two-mile climb to the top. In the spruce-fir forests hereabouts, a relatively common sight is the chickaree, a small squirrel that is reddish above and whitish below, with a black stripe separating the two colors. Another inhabitant of this forest, although less likely to be seen, is the marten, a weasel relative and a species endangered in this state.

A longer (and more strenuous) trail leads from the same parking lot up to a high pasture named **Bull-of-the-Woods** and past a mountain of the same name. This point is above the tree line, and alpine tundra stretches up the series of ridges that finally end at the top of Wheeler Peak. At the tree line, ptarmigans have been spotted. In talus slopes and in the tundra, yellow-bellied marmots and pikas are often seen, busily foraging or perched on a prominent rock. The latter animals are small, gray, and tailless, resembling guinea pigs but in fact related to rabbits. From the top of Wheeler Peak, the view is astounding, with rank after rank of snow-capped mountains stretching north in Colorado. Less traveled is the **Latir Peak Wilderness,** at the northern edge of this block of the Carson Forest. Several campsites, including ones at Cabresto Lake, provide access to the wilderness.

West of Taos, Route 64 passes over the

ABOVE: *Removed from the endangered species list in 1994, the bald eagle is making a comeback along southwestern rivers and streams. With its cousin, the golden eagle, it is the Indians' most honored bird.*

spectacular 650-foot-deep gorge of the Rio Grande, but that is dwarfed by the Brazos Box, visible from the Brazos Overlook, near milepost 144, and also from the junction of Routes 64 and 84 south of Chama. This steep-walled canyon of the Rio Brazos (meaning "swift river"), with ancient quartzite cliffs, is 2,000 feet deep, three times deeper than the Rio Grande near Taos.

North of Chama lies the **Edward Sargent Fish and Wildlife Management Area❖,** purchased originally by the Nature Conservancy and then by the state. It is 32 square miles of high rolling

39

RIGHT: *Icy meltwater plummets through a field of yellow-and-white alpine marsh marigolds in July. The flowers bloom 12,000 feet up, above the tree line on Wheeler Peak, New Mexico's highest mountain.*

BELOW: *Lichens and the last of the snow adorn the Carson National Forest's Wheeler Peak Wilderness. The area protects the blue gem of Horseshoe Lake, one of the few natural lakes in the state of New Mexico.*

upland, with meadows among aspens and oaks, streams, and a lake. Except for one road (Pine Street out of Chama), travel is on foot or by horseback. It is managed principally as range for elk, though hunters bag an occasional deer. In early times, elk were found in most of the mountainous areas of New Mexico, but by the turn of this century, they had been virtually wiped out from overhunting. A program of reintroducing elk from elsewhere began soon thereafter, and elk are now relatively abundant in some of their old haunts. Two spectacles coincide to make late September to mid-October the best time to visit: The aspens are turning gold, the oaks a variety of reds; and bull elk, mainlining testosterone right from the glands to the bloodstream, are gathering females into harems and proclaiming their own excellence by loud roars called bugling.

The Rio Chama arises in Colorado, and before entering the Rio Grande near the San Juan Pueblo, it creates three reservoirs—Heron, El Vado, and Abiquiu. Despite this domestication, the river provides excellent fishing, kayaking, rafting, and backpacking. Between Heron Lake and El Vado Lake and for three miles south of El Vado Dam is the **Rio Chama Wildlife and Fishing Area❖.** A trail follows the canyon between the two lakes. South of El Vado Lake the river enters a lovely gorge with steeply sloping, partly forested sides of red, orange, and brown rock, emerging at Abiquiu Lake 30 miles downstream. A state "scenic and pastoral river," it has also been designated part of the National Wild and Scenic River system. The first ten miles is a Bureau of Land Management wilderness study area. Thereafter it is the **Chama River Canyon Wilderness❖,** part of the Santa Fe National Forest.

Boating season is from mid-April through May, when the Chama overflows El Vado Dam, creating class I and II+ rapids, all relatively straightforward, for a peaceful two-day trip down the 900-foot-high canyon. In addition, irrigation releases often make river running possible again in July and August. The river meanders through ranchland from Abiquiu south to the confluence, and most boaters end their trip in a

---

OVERLEAF: *In autumn, riparian areas in Taos Canyon are ablaze with the gold of turning cottonwood and willow leaves, burnished all the brighter in shimmering shafts of fabled New Mexican light.*

41

ABOVE: *With Mesa Alta brooding on the horizon, the Chama River, a favorite of anglers, rafters, and other river rats, flows through a designated wilderness area on its way south to meet the Rio Grande.*

five-mile stretch north of the town and reservoir dam. In recent years, running the Chama has become sufficiently popular that new "hardened" campgrounds are being installed a few miles upstream of Abiquiu Dam. The number of boaters is restricted on the upper section, so spring permits should be requested from the BLM Taos office by December 31.

The road back to Chama, Route 84, is one of the most spectacular in the state. On the way is **Ghost Ranch Living Museum❖,** an interpretative center for the Carson National Forest whose exhibits on the flora, fauna, and geology of the region are mostly outdoors and alive. North of the museum, on the west side of the road, **Echo Amphitheater** has been carved (by wind and water) out of the stunning red, yellow, white, even purple rock. It is a good summer backdrop for the kestrels, white-throated swifts, and violet-green swallows that inhabit the cliffs, and it sends the sound of one's own voice bouncing off the rock.

About eight miles west of Chama on Route 64, all the watercourses tend to head for the Pacific Ocean; behind one at this point, they flow east to the Gulf of Mexico. That phenomenon explains how the curvilinear line down the map called the Continental Divide is determined. Less than 20 miles beyond that, just past the town of Dulce, Jicarilla Route 8 (J8) heads south to **Stone Lake❖** and several other natural lakes of the Jicarilla Apache, generally taken to be the highlight of bird-watching in north-central New Mexico and well plied by fishermen. A bit more than 16 miles south of Dulce a dirt road runs east (left) and skirts the northern edge of Stone Lake, passing through a plethora of burrows making up a working prairie dog "town." The road ends on high ground above the lake—an excellent spot to stroll along the shore looking for western grebes. Or travel south on J8 to the southern rim of the lake, where another road leads to an abandoned lodge, beyond which a dirt road goes to a marshy area where a patient soul can peer through the reeds for soras and Virginia rails.

South of Stone Lake, J8 (now dirt) meets Route 95, which heads back east between two other lakes, **Buford** and **Hayden,** the former an outstanding place for waterfowl in summer and migrating birds in season. Hundreds of pairs of nesting grebes are active there in midsummer months. If there has been a recent rain, it is best to backtrack to Dulce; otherwise, Route 95 continues on to **Heron Lake State Park❖.** There are campsites and 20-pound lake trout lurking in the depths of the lake, and the ponderosa pines ringing it give it the appearance of a natural lake.

THE PLATEAU

A bit west of where Route 64 exits the last section of the Carson National Forest onto the Colorado Plateau, a gentle but noticeable feature becomes apparent to the south among the mesas and hills. It is **Gobernador Knob,** or what the Navajo call Choolii, the place where First Man and First Woman found the baby that would become one of the most beloved Navajo gods, Changing Woman, and a landform of central spiritual significance to the tribe.

Detouring about a half-hour south from Farmington on Route 371 brings the **Bisti Wilderness❖** into view. A primitive road leads up to the edge of the badlands, an utterly eerie, silent place of eroded clay beds and sandstone—mostly various shades of gray, but highlighted with red and yellow and streaked black with the occasional seam of coal. Here and there, a remnant of shale caprock has protected the softer material, creating hoodoos, pinnacles, arches, and forms that look like mushrooms.

The road to the edge is best tried with a four-wheel drive, and not right after a summer rain (which turns this country into mush). Winter snow and mud can also be deterrents. Vehicles, including bicycles, are prohibited, but a faint trail leads into the badlands from the parking lot alongside a fence and then past a mine. Keeping the mine in sight, one can wander the badlands without getting lost in what seems a jumbled, tortured maze (if lost, walk west to hit Route 371).

East of the Bisti Wilderness is yet another realm of badlands, **De-Na-Zin Wilderness❖.** It lies along County Route 7500, which runs northeast from Route 371 and connects with Route 44 at Huerfano Trading Post. Here one finds mesas, dry washes, spires, and bluffs in a variety of colors ranging from yellow to purple. South of the Bisti Badlands, and best approached by driving through De-Na-Zin and then south on Routes 44 and 57, is **Chaco Culture National Historical Park❖.** Here the most enigmatic ruins in North America lie brooding in the sun, amid an enormity of empty, arid space. Long ago, a high civilization flourished here in multistoried buildings of flat stone with hundreds of rooms and ceremonial centers. The Chaco culture was a major part of the greater Anasazi cultures that seemed to have vanished about A.D. 1300. Most archaeologists today agree that they simply moved on (for reasons unclear) and wound up as the modern Hopi, Zuni, and Pueblo tribes along the Rio Grande. Among the many widely spaced ruins, Pueblo Bonito is a large hemispherical structure that contained hundreds of rooms and numerous round structures that were certainly *kivas,* underground places for ceremonies, entered by ladders from above. Pueblo Bonito appears to have been built as an enormous passive-solar habitation, making extraordinarily well worked out use of the daily and seasonal passage of the sun overhead for purposes of heating and cooling. Chaco is also the home of the famous "sun dagger," a recently discovered calendrical device whereby the summer solstice sun cast a dagger of light directly in the middle of a spiral etched into the stone atop a high butte. Since the sun dagger's discovery in the 1970s, one of the massive stone slabs that helped create this light-and-shadow phenomenon has

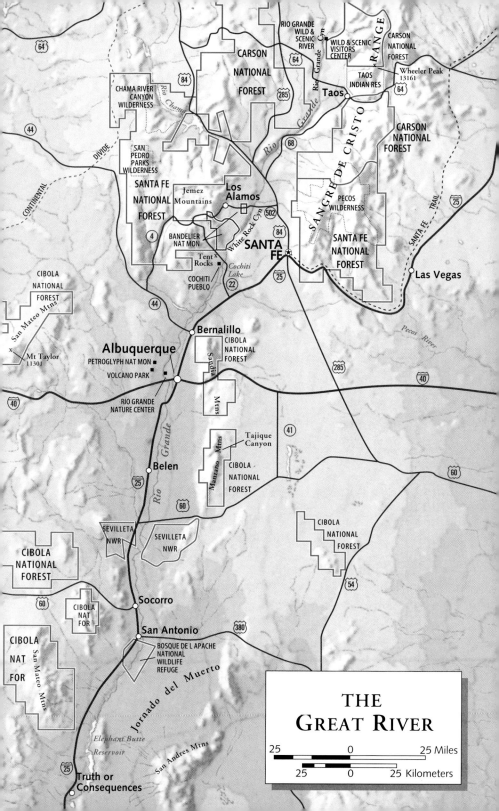

THE
GREAT RIVER

25   0   25 Miles

25   0   25 Kilometers

11 miles down between Socorro and Belen. The magma is pushing the crust upward at a rate of about eight inches a century, suggesting a change of course for the Rio Grande sometime in the distant future.

For now, however, the Great River—from the place where it sluices into New Mexico to a marshy midpoint south of Socorro—provides the state with some of its finest natural areas. South of Elephant Butte Reservoir, the river is chiefly an agricultural benefit, watering (among others) the fields near Hatch, the chili center of the universe. Chili, New Mexicans stoutly believe, is this hemisphere's greatest contribution to the world, on a par with the tomato, potato, and constitutional democracy.

NORTHERN WHITEWATER

Paid fresh tribute in spring and early summer by the snow-fed mountain streams of Colorado, the **Rio Grande Wild and Scenic River❖**, managed by the Bureau of Land Management, makes its debut in New Mexico between April and June in a rush that excites the hearts of kayakers and rafters. Two hundred feet below the rim of the gorge it has carved from alternating beds of lava and compacted gravel, it will descend in 24 miles to a depth of 800 feet near the confluence of the Red River. For the first 12 miles, it is considered class I and II in the International Whitewater Rating System, meaning that its rapids (occasional) are small, with waves up to 3 feet high. Thereafter, only experienced kayakers will be able to handle the class V rapids (and one unrunnable class VI section) that occur deep in the boulder-strewn gorge of the upper Taos Box Canyon. Along the way, the river is graced with pines, willows, horsetails and Apache plumes, various cacti, wildflowers, and, although it is increasingly popular among river rats, relatively few people. (Permits from the Bureau of Land Management are required for running the river.)

Access to this portion of the river is from Lobatos Bridge in Colorado or, some twelve miles south of the border, via Route 378, which heads west and riverward about four miles north of the town of Questa, New Mexico. There is a visitor center where Route 378 reach-

LEFT: On a torrent of melted snow, compliments of Colorado tributaries, white-water rafters ply the northern reaches of the Great River from April to June. Here they plummet through Taos Box.

es the edge of the river gorge, and a paved road along the rim offers many campsites and hiking trails. The lower Taos Box, south of Dunn's Bridge, offers class III rapids through a majestic gorge that, below the Taos Junction Bridge, opens out into a canyon. Here, just below the bridge, is **Orilla Verde Recreation Area❖,** a good camping site reachable off Route 68 from Taos. This road snakes alongside the river, one of the state's highly scenic drives, passing such old, Oz-like river hamlets as Pilar. Indeed, to drive south from Taos to Santa Fe in the late afternoon is to be immersed in an incomparable show of New Mexico light and landform.

West of Pojoaque pueblo on Route 502, Otowi Bridge crosses the river and from here south, in **White Rock Canyon,** is a highly popular stretch of class II water that leads into **Cochiti Lake❖,** a ten-mile-long body of water created by the construction of a huge earthen dam. Since it came into being in the 1970s, the lake has been a popular recreational spot, particularly for boaters and anglers. A campground is operated by the nearby Cochiti pueblo, located a mile or so south of Cochiti Dam on Route 85 and dominated by a water tower painted to resemble an Indian drum, for which the Cochiti craftspeople are renowned.

THE RIVER'S ROCKY FLANKS

Off Route 85, in the approximate middle of the spread-out Cochiti pueblo (a word that means town, not necessarily a multistoried adobe structure as at Taos or, anciently, Chaco), the dirt Forest Road 266 heads northwest. In five miles one comes upon **Tent Rocks❖,** a little-visited and eerie array of nearly mosquelike formations, round and tapered, often with little "hats" of resistant rock perched on their tops. Made of claylike volcanic tuff, and differentially eroded along vertical joints to become an army of tall cones at parade rest, they are studded with the small pieces of black volcanic glass sometimes called Apache tears. Rising up from pinyon-juniper woodland that also hosts the northernmost stands of the shrub called pointleaf manzanita, these

---

RIGHT: *At dusk in the high plains west of Taos, the world is nothing but sagebrush, sky, silence, and the Sangre de Cristo Mountains.*

OVERLEAF: *Glorieta Mesa and a well-decorated cholla cactus welcome the morning sun in the Santa Fe National Forest near Pecos.*

"tepees" afford fascinating shapes and mini-canyons to hike among, gentle views of distant mountains, and a fine arena (maintained by the Bureau of Land Management) for a picnic with rarely another soul in sight. Tread lightly here, because Tent Rocks is presently deemed a Natural Area of Critical Environmental Concern.

As it flows through White Creek Canyon, the great river is flanked by one of the most popular recreation areas in the state, the **Santa Fe National Forest❖;** this forest includes several ranges—in particular the lower end of the Sangre de Cristo Mountains to the east and the Jemez Mountains to the west—which in turn contain several wilderness areas. Their popularity derives largely from their location within an hour's drive of Santa Fe and Albuquerque, home to more than one third of the state's population. Many of these 600,000 residents are bent on hiking, skiing, fishing, backpacking, and other outdoor activities. The great variety of habitat, ranging from pinyon-juniper lands to tundra, also makes this forest a favorite for birders.

Like any natural area of more than 1.5 million acres that lies near population centers, the accessible places within it are much used, while one can find solitude in the remote and inaccessible parts. For example, the heavily forested **Pecos Wilderness❖**—some 240,000 acres northeast of Santa Fe and Pecos in the Sangre de Cristos—is the forest's most often visited wilderness, offering more than 30 entry points and much day hiking near its edges. But in the rugged canyons and steep mountains within its interior, the serious backpacker can get happily lost in a wild realm that seems nearly untouched, full of lakes (15) and mountain streams, pine and spruce forests—even bristlecone pines.

Quite different is the **San Pedro Parks Wilderness❖,** across the Rio Grande Rift in the Jemez Mountains. Far smaller than the Pecos Wilderness—less than 50,000 acres—it is a place of high grassy parks and meadows with spruce and other conifer stands. A large portion of the entire Jemez division is slated to become a national recreation area, which typically means further accommodations for the kinds of use—such as trailer hookups—that purists sniff at. But while pressure will continue to

RIGHT: *The Truchas Peaks (meaning "trout" in Spanish) loom craggily above the soaring spruces, cold waters, and intensely green high meadows of the Pecos Wilderness in the Santa Fe National Forest.*

ABOVE LEFT: *In the short growing season of the mountains, western yarrow, wild mint, and paintbrush are among the highland wildflowers that make their miraculous appearance each year without fail.*

grow along with the state's major population center, the area will still provide the intimate and the spectacular, even all in a day's work.

One example of many is the drive from Albuquerque to St. Peter's Dome Lookout. Going northeast on Route 4, out of the town of San Ysidro on Route 44, one soon enters a wide canyon flanked by rocky mesas that turn an increasingly bright and deep red as the canyon narrows and the road passes through the funky little town of Jemez Springs—noted for its hot springs. North of town is Soda Dam, a huge convoluted plug of travertine till being laid down by the hot, mineralized waters of the Jemez River. At the base of the "dam" only a few feet from the road is a pool of hot water in which locals and visitors often sit. Across the road is a cliff of red granite, at two billion years of age some of the oldest exposed rock in the region. Beyond, up in the mountains, inviting trails lead off here and there along old and neglect-

Above: *Mist envelops the rocks in the lower falls of Bandelier National Monument's Frijoles Canyon, a lodestar for modern-day hikers and backpackers and once home to ancient Anasazi pueblo dwellers.*

ed logging roads to sudden, breathtaking overlooks of deep canyons and mountains that turn from green to blue.

Roadcuts along Route 4 are covered with tiny whitish-gray balls called popcorn lava, signaling that this is volcano country. Before long, off to the north, a vast grassy plain stretches away. The Valle Grande is the interior of a huge caldera resulting from an enormous volcanic explosion that created much of the substructure of today's landscape in the Jemez Mountains about a million years ago. In all, some 75 cubic miles of glowing ash flowed onto the land and cooled, later to be cut and sculpted by streams into a mountain range. In the caldera (which is now part of private landholdings dating back to Spanish times), archaeologists have found stone blinds from which locals have hunted deer for some 5,000 years.

Not far beyond the last sight of the caldera, Forest Road 289 heads south through ponderosa and spruce forests, tantalizing vistas of distant mountains, and in summer, delightful glimpses of red penstemon, the favorite of hummingbirds. Each plant features a series of stalks, like the stays on a sailboat, with red pennants hanging bravely in the breeze. Eventually, after about six miles, Forest Road 142 branches off to the east, leading another half-dozen rough miles to St. Peter's Dome Lookout. Here the world spreads out—the columnar cliffs of Capulin Canyon, the Rio Grande, Cochiti Lake, alpine summits, plateaus, mesa lands stretching to an unimaginable horizon. Four-wheel drives are highly recommended on both routes, which are closed in the winter.

Just below the lookout to the east, **Bandelier National Monument❖** wilderness spreads out across the **Pajarito Plateau.** Known principally for the old Indian dwellings found there in the nineteenth century and first documented by a Swiss-born archaeologist named Bandelier, two thirds of the area (about 23,000 acres) has been set aside as a roadless wilderness. This is cut by several streams in deep canyons, most notably Frijoles Creek, which descends through Frijoles Canyon to meet the Rio Grande in White Rock Canyon. In this lush riparian area, cottonwoods, box elders, and shrubbery, along with less frequent water birches, provide habitat for a multitude of songbirds in summer and for small mammals such as the tassel-eared Abert's squirrel and raccoons, along with bobcats, foxes, and coyotes. Many visitors follow the trail from the visitor center into Frijoles Canyon and explore the old dwellings carved in the volcanic tuff some 700 years ago by the presumed ancestors of the Cochiti Indians. One of these ruins, called Long House, contains the remains of more than 350 rooms, and in a cave above, some 12,000 Mexican free-tail bats have taken up summer residence. Old dwellings cut out of the cliff face seem wondrous enough. It is perhaps more amazing to realize that this canyon, from 400 to 1,200 feet deep, was almost entirely carved by water from a vast layer of the ejecta from the caldera now called Valle Grande. That is a lot of ash.

Climbing up out of the canyon, one encounters pinyon-juniper woodlands with ponderosas and oaks here and there. Above that, 8,000 feet up in the foothills of the Jemez, mixed conifer forest takes over, home for elk, mountain lions, and black bears—the latter two rarely seen. The highest point in the monument at 10,199 feet, Cerro Grande was formerly a montane grassland but is now forested with

Douglas firs and ponderosas, the result of fire suppression policies. In 1977, a fire burned 15,000 acres of the monument and, while the scars are still visible along Route 4, it inaugurated a modern policy of controlled burns for the management of this fragile ecosystem.

THE SANDIA MOUNTAINS

Towering as high as a mile above Albuquerque, the **Sandia Mountains❖** are one of the most used and accessible natural areas in the state. Part of the eclectic **Cibola National Forest❖,** they are the result of a massive 22-mile-long fault block that lifted up at this point along the Rio Grande Rift, creating a rugged western slope of naked cliffs and pinnacles steep enough for hang gliders, and a more gradually sloping eastern side covered with forest. Two roads, one from Placitas to the north and one from San Antonito in the east, climb to the 10,676-foot crest, leading from Sonoran grasslands and pinyon-juniper forests through transitional ponderosa pines, to Douglas firs and other conifers, Engelmann spruces, and corkbark firs in less than an hour's ride from Albuquerque. A trip to the Sandia Crest via the west face is even faster—a 15-minute tram ride (north of the city limits off Tramway Boulevard, billed as the longest tram in the world). There one finds a visitor center, a restaurant, a ski area, a small forest of radio and TV towers, astounding views, and a wilderness area crisscrossed by more than a hundred miles of trails on which, despite the more than 1.5 million visits a year to the mountains, one can walk or cross-country ski without seeing more than a dozen people. Instead, one might see mule deer or black bears (which in drought seasons, unfortunately, find their way into downtown Albuquerque).

There are a number of trails for hiking up into the Sandias, two of which leave from the Juan Tabo Picnic Ground on Forest Road 333, which runs northeast from Tramway Boulevard. The most popular of these (and of all trails in the Sandias) is also the most strenuous: **La Luz Trail,** which rises from about 7,000 feet up the towering cliffs to the crest in about seven and a half miles. After a mile of gradual rise, it is all

---

OVERLEAF: *Looming 5,000 feet above the Rio Grande valley, the Sandia Mountains, seen here from Coronado State Park, were a stopping-off place for the Spanish explorer Coronado almost five centuries ago.*

ABOVE: *A mountain lion, created between A.D. 1300 and 1650, is among the petroglyphs pecked in Rinconada Canyon's lava rocks in Petroglyph National Monument, which overlooks the nearby city of Albuquerque.*

switchbacks, and about three miles up, the trail crosses a canyon formed by the Rincon Ridge. After that point, various paths lead off to rock faces where human flies ply their craft. Seven miles up, the **Crest Spur Trail** runs a strenuous half-mile to Sandia Crest, and La Luz goes another mile to the tramway. For most, this is a highly aerobic one-day hike, but there are those of great lung and sinew who enter footraces up La Luz.

Perhaps because of their proximity to the city, some people let themselves think that the Sandias are not dangerous like other mountains. But every year a handful of people with their guard down topple off even much-traveled La Luz Trail or attempt rock faces that are beyond their ability, or simply get lost, sometimes to their mortal regret.

A less strenuous outing in Albuquerque is to the **Rio Grande Nature Center State Park❖,** at the end of Candelaria Road off Rio Grande Boulevard. This state park is a small wildlife refuge among the thick cottonwoods of the Rio Grande's bosque, a pleasant spot for relaxed birding. A small pond attracts a variety of waterfowl in season, exhibits in an excellent visitor center detail the life of the bosque, and several trails through the woods lead to river's edge. Birders are encouraged to let the visitor center know what birds they have seen.

Forming a familiar feature on the horizon west of the city are five ancient volcanic cones on top of the western mesa in the grasslands. These and the surrounding 5,000 acres were purchased by the Land and Water Conservation Fund and since 1976 have been managed by the city as **Volcano Park❖.** Here one is amid desert grassland—blue and black grama grasses—yuccas, cacti, sage, and four-wing saltbush. Coyotes, kit foxes, hawks, and turkey vultures patrol the area at night, and the silence of the day is often shattered by the loud, brassy song of rock wrens. To reach this peaceful spot take Route 149 north off Interstate 40 west of Albuquerque and travel 4.5 miles north on Paseo del Volcan.

South of the Sandia Mountains lies a sister range, the **Manzano Mountains,** also a part of the Cibola National Forest. About an hour's drive south of Albuquerque, down Route 337 from the town of Tijeras and then west on Route 55, lies a canyon where, in season, even a Vermonter will be impressed. On maps it is called **Tajique Canyon❖;** locally it is known as Fourth of July Canyon for the tradition of celebrating that day. But the floral fireworks occur in October, for here, almost uniquely in the state, the soil, altitude, and other conditions are perfect for the growth of various western species of maple trees. A well-marked trail leads one up through what must be the most crimson place in New Mexico—but as in show business, timing is everything. The canyon is at the end of Forest Road 55, a winding and well-marked service road that heads west out of Tajique.

DESERT AND MARSH

Interstate 25 south from Albuquerque toward Socorro runs through land that, away from the river, looks like desert, with sage and creosote bush and, here and there, naked dunes. But these were once desert *grasslands:* A century of overgrazing has brought them to their present condition. The northernmost region of true Chihuahuan Desert

OVERLEAF: *Seemingly on signal, thousands of snow geese fill the sky above Bosque del Apache National Wildlife Refuge along the Rio Grande. The refuge is a wintering ground for sandhill cranes as well.*

really occurs in the neighborhood of Socorro, and one of the best places to explore it is the **Presilla Wilderness Study Area❖,** lying east of the Rio Grande and maintained by the Bureau of Land Management. At Escondida, just north of Socorro, a road bridges the river, and at the little community of Pueblito, Quebradas Road goes south into a land of dunes, canyons, and benchlands cut through by arroyos. To the east are rough, multicolored desert mountains, the **Sierra de las Canas** (the Breaks), rising to 6,200 feet.

Local residents come to the Presilla to climb, hunt deer and quail, and hike among the typical Chihuahuan Desert plants—creosote bush, mesquite, cholla and prickly pear cactus, mariola, and here and there ocotillo. One of the arroyos that descend from the mountains and slice across the Presilla, **Arroyo del Tajo,** bears many Indian pictographs and has been incorporated into a Natural Area of Critical Environmental Concern. Like many sites where the progenitors of today's Indian people have left their marks, this one is subject to vandalism by thoughtless people. The state and federal governments are seeking ways to protect such places from desecration (by increased educational programs, for example), but a sad solution may have to be limiting visitation. It is useful to think of such places as someone's church. To the north of the Presilla area is the **Sevilleta National Wildlife Refuge,** a research location closed to the public; to the south is one of the most famous wildlife refuges in the region.

One of the grandest spectacles in the Southwest is to be seen on a winter afternoon looking west from the tour loop road in **Bosque del Apache National Wildlife Refuge❖.** There in the grassy marshlands, on some indeterminable signal, thousands upon thousands of flashing white snow geese take to the air, wheeling and crying out, almost obscuring the Magdalena Mountains to the west, filling the icy blue sky. Among them can be seen the smaller Ross' geese, and they will all be joined by thousands of sandhill cranes, pink in the sun, emitting their haunting burble. And amid this throng may be a few larger, white birds—a handful of whooping cranes. In all, 100,000 birds might be in the air at one time.

To reach the refuge, drive nine miles south of Socorro on Interstate 25 and turn east to San Antonio. From there, Route 1 heads south and within about three miles the refuge begins, although headquarters (with excellent interpretive material and exhibits) is another four miles on.

While much of the refuge is desert upland east and west of the Rio Grande, the main draw is 7,000 intensively managed acres of riparian land along the river. In 1986, after decades of low budgets and relative neglect, the Fish and Wildlife Service determined to make the refuge a showcase, bringing the water ditches, dikes, and canals from the river back up to snuff; adding interpretive material and viewing platforms; rooting out the pesky tamarisk trees (or salt cedars), a weedy introduced species; and planting more than 12,000 cottonwoods and 6,000 black willows. The result is an astonishingly diverse habitat of marsh, lake, woodland, meadow, and farmland surrounded by desert, and a bird list of about 300 species (and some 60 mammal species) to match it. Arrays of ducks (including the Mexican mallard) and other water birds and shorebirds put in here, along with raptors from eagles to kestrels, numerous songbirds, and various flycatchers, quail, and nighthawks. Even jaegers, kittiwakes, and other marine birds have been known to make an occasional, if wholly accidental, stop. Worth a trip at any time of year (though mosquitoes are brazen from May through August) and very heavily visited, the refuge presents as its main attraction, of course, the winter population of snow geese and cranes.

The whoopers are the result of an experiment, whereby eggs from captive pairs of whooping cranes were put in the nests of sandhills in their Idaho breeding grounds. The whooping cranes double-clutch: When their egg is taken, they produce another. In addition to producing more young this way, researchers hoped that the foster whoopers would take amorous note of one another, mate, and establish a burgeoning second migratory route for this severely endangered crane. By 1992, the experiment had apparently failed and eggs were no longer being sneaked into sandhill nests, but the refuge remains one of the best places anywhere to get an intimate glimpse of these birds. And during the migrations in late October and February, New Mexicans who live along the Rio Grande north of the refuge keep an ear cocked for the distant burble of the sandhills, heard long before the birds are visible. Then, day after day, swirling ribbons and Vs of sunlit cranes materialize out of the cobalt sky. Calling and spiraling to gain altitude, they sweep across the heavens and disappear. Their journey along the great river has been going on since long before humans were around to be awed by such glorious steadfastness.

BADLANDS AND OASES: SOUTHEASTERN NEW MEXICO

El Camino Real (the royal highway established by the Spanish conquistadores) led through a flat, unforgiving region called Jornada del Muerto. Little but windblown sand and clay and lava rock, it was described in the 1840s as a "long and dreary waste." Stretching south from Route 380, which crosses from San Antonio to Carrizozo, it is almost entirely within the White Sands Missile Range, although the Bureau of Land Management maintains a 30,000-acre piece of it, reachable via County Routes 2268 and 2322. In July 1945, scientists came across a wholly new mineral in Jornada del Muerto, about 20 miles south of Route 380. A green, jadelike material, it was called Trinitite: sand fused into glass by the detonation of the first atomic bomb, on July 16, 1945, at a site called Trinity. Leaving a crater 8 feet deep and 400 yards in diameter, the explosion broke windows 120 miles away in Silver City. In Albuquerque the earth trembled. And worldwide the affairs of humanity were irrevocably altered. It is ironic that New Mexico—the home still of some of the most ancient and spiritual people in the nation, the Pueblo Indians, whose origins are in the land's holy places—also played host to humanity's Faustian bargain

LEFT: *At the White Sands National Monument the eerie dead white of gypsum takes on the pastels of dusk in an area called Heart of the Dunes; in the distance the San Andres Mountains rise in the west.*

with the atom, perhaps the defining moment of modern times.

A glance at the map—and certainly a glance at the road across Jornada del Muerto—suggests that the southeastern part of New Mexico is a vast, empty region with but a few places suitable for human habitation. Indeed, only some 150,000 people live in its seven counties, an area of about 30,000 square miles. By contrast, some eight *million* people live in New Jersey, while southeastern New Mexico has the space for four New Jerseys. But this is not simply empty land; the area shares richly in the natural diversity of the state. There are badlands, dunes, and lava flows; rugged mountains carpeted with old forest; canyons, springs, and rivers; and, of course, the geopoetry of limestone caves, of which those near Carlsbad are the most famous. Carlsbad Caverns are located in Eddy County—itself a model of New Mexican diversity with elevations ranging from about 3,000 to nearly 8,000 feet, floodplains, limestone and gypsum foothills, grasslands, shin oak stands, mountains, creeks, canyons, and the Pecos River—in all, habitat for more than 370 species of birds, which is more than half of all found in North America.

BADLANDS

Less than a thousand years ago **Little Black Peak,** which lies a dozen miles north of Carrizozo, emitted successive flows of ropy, shiny lava that spread out, mostly southward, to form what today is a 44-mile "river" of black *malpais* (bad land) across what had long before been an inland sea. This is one of the most recent and best preserved such flows in the contiguous 48 states. The lava surged into the lowest elevations, creating domes and blisters, pressure ridges, caves, tubes, and deep fissures where it cooled and shrank—a place described as "a burnt pepperoni pizza long forgotten in Paul Bunyan's oven."

The lava could not cover higher ridges, and one of these, along Route 380, is the **Valley of Fires Recreation Area❖.** From there a 45-minute walk along an interpretative trail takes visitors among the bizarre shapes of the *malpais.* Not all *mal,* however: Enough soil, blown by the wind, has lodged in crevices in the black basalt to provide homes here and there for prickly pear and cholla cacti, sotols, tufts of grama grass, even junipers. Mule deer and coyotes live here, though they are seldom seen. Small desert rodents and lizards may also appear—the latter typically with darker-than-normal skin. The

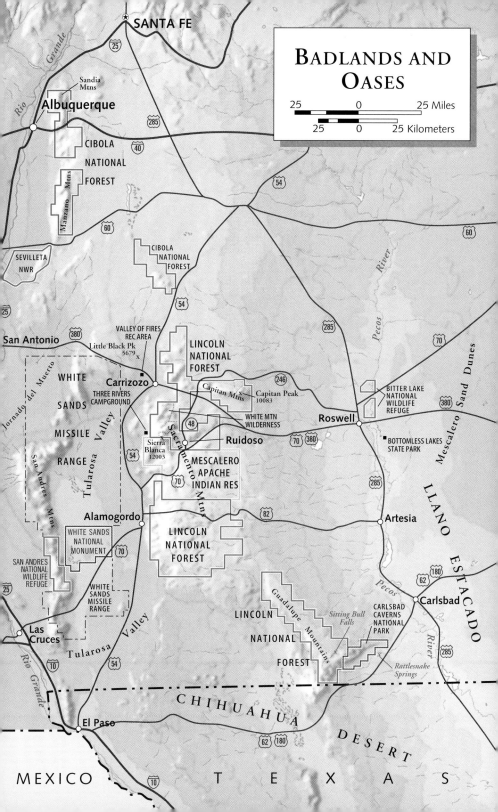

BADLANDS AND OASES

25   0   25 Miles

25   0   25 Kilometers

SANTA FE

Rio Grande

25

Sandia Mtns

Albuquerque

CIBOLA

NATIONAL

FOREST

285

40

Manzano Mtns

60

54

60

SEVILLETA NWR

CIBOLA NATIONAL FOREST

25

54

285

Pecos River

VALLEY OF FIRES REC AREA

San Antonio

380

Little Black Pk
5679 x

LINCOLN

NATIONAL

FOREST

70

Bitter Lake National Wildlife Refuge

Mescalero Sand Dunes

WHITE

Carrizozo

246

THREE RIVERS CAMPGROUND

Capitan Mtns x

Capitan Peak
10083

380

SANDS

Roswell

MISSILE

48

WHITE MTN WILDERNESS

70   380

San Andres Mtns

RANGE

54

Sierra Blanca
12003

Ruidoso

Sacramento Mtns

BOTTOMLESS LAKES STATE PARK

Jornado del Muerto

Tularosa Valley

MESCALERO

APACHE

INDIAN RES

70

285

LLANO

Alamogordo

82

Artesia

25

WHITE SANDS NATIONAL MONUMENT

70

LINCOLN

NATIONAL

FOREST

ESTACADO

SAN ANDRES NATIONAL WILDLIFE REFUGE

WHITE SANDS MISSILE RANGE

180

Pecos

62

Las Cruces

25

Tularosa

Valley

54

LINCOLN

NATIONAL

FOREST

Guadalupe Mountains

Sitting Bull Falls

CARLSBAD CAVERNS NATIONAL PARK

Carlsbad

River

285

Rattlesnake Springs

Rio Grande

10

CHIHUAHUA

El Paso

DESERT

62   180

MEXICO

10

T E X A S

same species tend to be lighter farther south, where the black lava gives way to alabaster dunes.

The snow-white desert of **White Sands National Monument✣** defies common sense. Lying about 15 miles southwest of Alamogordo north of Route 70, it simply seems *too white,* glistening and sparkling under the blue sky like some strange land from science fiction. This is gypsum sand (technically, the mineral selenite), and the world's largest gypsum dune field, containing some eight billion tons of gypsum, enough to supply the United States with wallboard and plaster for nearly a millennium. Half of the dune field—some 275 square miles—is within the monument, forming the most spectacular feature of the large, sun-drenched Tularosa Valley, a great basin between the San Andres (west) and Sacramento (east) mountain ranges. There is no outlet from the

Tularosa Valley; any water that finds its way there from the surrounding mountains and ridges either percolates into the desert or evaporates.

The two mountain ranges were once the flanks of a great uplifted dome that included in its innards a 500-foot layer of gypsum, the result of the evaporation of inland seas before the period of uplift. About ten million years ago, the center of the dome, a block bounded by faults, dropped down thousands of feet, exposing the gypsum layer in the flanking mountain ranges. Erosion brought gypsum down into vast lakes in the basin that in turn evaporated, leaving dry playas (alkaline flats) of gypsum and salts. Much of the gypsum permeated the groundwater, and even today it percolates upward via capillary action into Lake Lucero to the southwest, forming jagged, daggerlike crystals of selenite on the shore. These crystals crack in the temperature extremes of the desert, and the sand-laden southwest winds of spring etch them into fine grains, adding them to the dunes that move northeastward at up to 33 feet a year. To visit the monument in the windy spring is to experience gypsum with all the senses, including taste.

Especially strong and shifting winds create circular dome-shaped dunes. Less vigorous winds create transverse rows of dunes, sloping gently on the

ABOVE: *Sand verbena is one of the handful of desert plants (including mesquite and snakeweed) that can survive in the grand selenite ocean of White Sands National Monument. This gypsum field covers more than 250 square miles and is still moving northeastward at a rate of about 30 feet a year, driven by the winds of spring.*

LEFT: *One horn of a barchan dune makes curvilinear magic in the crystalline desert moonscape, a scene that has served as an inspiration to a host of science fiction writers.*

upwind side, steeply on the downwind side, where the sand falls in mini-avalanches. Another dune form is called barchan, crescent-shaped hills with the horns pointing away from the wind. And where vegetation anchors some of the sand along the margins of the dune field, the wind creates U-shaped, parabolic dunes, concave on the upwind side.

This grand oceanic procession can all be seen along a 16-mile round-trip scenic drive that leads from the visitor center at the entrance into an area called the Heart of the Dunes. (The center includes a garden exhibiting the desert plants that can survive in gypsum—such as skunkbush sumac, Indian ricegrass, hoary rosemary mint, Rio Grande cottonwood, and soap tree yucca.) Five miles into the drive is a parking lot and a marked trail to a campsite. Seeing the dunes in moonlight and at sunrise is eerily akin to being on another planet.

The monument lies within the White Sands Missile Range and is closed when the military uses the range for testing. Some 3,200 square miles of prime Chihuahuan Desert basin land in the missile range have been restricted altogether since the 1940s. Here pronghorns and oryx are abundant. The latter, an African species, was ill-advisedly introduced some years back and now sometimes threatens plant life at the monument. The **San Andres National Wildlife Refuge**—west of the monument in the San Andres Mountains and off limits to all but researchers and wildlife managers—is host to a rich array of wildlife, including desert mule deer, mountain lions, and bighorn sheep. These animals occasionally wander out of the missile range and have been seen ambling innocently across Route 70. Some observers consider the refuge an ideal place to reintroduce to the wild the Mexican gray wolf, currently an endangered subspecies found only in captivity. Others, including the military, disagree, and the matter remains controversial.

THE SACRAMENTOS

The Sacramento Mountains, which close off the Tularosa Valley to the east and comprise most of the **Lincoln National Forest❖,** contain

---

RIGHT: *Lit by the afternoon sun, stands of evergreens and aspens sweep to the horizon in a vista from the summit of Monjeau Peak, one of the Sacramento Mountains in the White Mountain Wilderness.*

numerous subranges, some of the finest skiing and other outdoor recreation in the Southwest, and a great deal of Old West hoopla and history. It was here, in the now restored town of Lincoln, that Billy the Kid hung out and warred in the last years of his short life, and here that a large number of the wide-ranging Apache finally fetched up—in the Mescalero Apache Reservation. The Sacramentos dominate the landscape of this region, visible from as far off as the Texas border.

The dominant peak is **Sierra Blanca,** which rears up east of **Three Rivers Campground** to a height of 12,003 feet, making it the highest mountain in the state outside of the Sangre de Cristos to the north. More to the point, it rises 7,800 feet above the surround, the greatest relief in the state; a popular, strenuous 9-mile hike to its crest leads to subalpine tundra and a vista that seems to stretch forever. From the summit, one can see the Guadalupe Mountains of Texas to the south, the Sangre de Cristos to the north, and the Gilas to the west. Sierra Blanca's summit is in Apacheland and is best approached by driving from Tularosa through the town of Mescalero (where Apache tribal headquarters will provide permission for the climb). Then proceed north of Ruidoso to Route 532 and a spectacular mountain drive of 12 miles through Lincoln National Forest to a small parking lot just before the main parking lot at Ski Apache.

From there, the trail meanders up through Douglas firs five feet in diameter, grassy valleys, over the crest of Lookout Mountain, and to the (in summer) densely flowered but still cold tundra of the crest. To the north lies the **White Mountain Wilderness,** an appealing area of nearly 50,000 acres athwart a long mountain ridge with more than 50 miles of trails, some of which rise into spruce and fir country.

North in the Capitan Mountains (unusual in that they run east-west), after a 1950s fire, foresters found a partly burned young black bear cub clinging to a tree. The bear, patched up and sent to the National Zoo in Washington, D.C., was dubbed Smokey and chosen to symbolize the National Forests and remind visitors to prevent forest fires Smokey was the most popular exhibit ever at the zoo until the pandas

---

LEFT: *A glorious eruption of Colorado four-o'clocks glows in the late spring sun of Salinas Pueblo Missions National Monument, home to three separate ruins of villages that existed into the Spanish era.*

arrived—so popular that he needed his own secretary to answer all the mail directed to him.

The eastern section of the Capitans, visible from the distant Texas border beyond the New Mexico plains, beckons forcefully to the sinewy backpacker. The various trails that rise to the summit of Capitan Peak, a 10,000-footer, are among the least trammeled places in the state, leading through dense forests of old-growth Douglas fir and spruces. Such solitude still exists here for precisely the same reason that the old-growth forest remains. The area proved too steep and rugged for logging and is too tough for all but the hardiest backpackers.

ABOVE: *A solitary frequenter of montane forests, the porcupine (from the Latin* porcus spina, *or prickly pig) survives in all New Mexico habitats, including the desert, by feeding on the cambium of woody plants and trees.*

RIGHT: *The black bear (which also comes in brown and cinnamon) is common in New Mexico forests, though rarely encountered.*

EAST OF THE PECOS

East of the Capitans, near Roswell and the Pecos River, is more gypsum country. Just across the river, Route 409 heads south through pastures that provide harborage for Sprague's pipit, a dry-land relative of the water pipit. Beyond lies **Bottomless Lakes State Park❖,** which includes an interesting series of sinkholes caused when gypsum and salt formations in solution with water simply collapsed. Some play host to the barking frog and, while not bottomless (a bit of harmless, New Mexico exaggeration), a few of them are a remarkable 90 feet deep.

The chief natural attraction near Roswell lies to the north and east, reached by East Pine Lodge Road: **Bitter Lake National Wildlife Refuge❖.**

Visitors are greeted at the entrance by burrowing owls and prairie dogs, and in its 24,500 acres of varied wildlife habitat in the Pecos River bottomlands, one can see large concentrations of waterfowl (including snow and Ross' geese) and sandhill cranes during the fall and winter. In the spring and fall a great variety of shorebirds and songbirds pass through the refuge, and its small colony of least terns make it this endangered bird's only New Mexico breeding locale.

Forty miles east of Roswell on Route 380 is Mescalero Ridge, an escarpment of red rock. Beyond that lie New Mexico's vast flat plains called Llano Estacado—oil country, peppered with nodding oil rigs and windmills all the way to Texas. Just below and east of the ridge, straddling the highway, are 60 miles of looming, light-tan dunes of fine quartz sand, the **Mescalero Sand Dunes❖.** The **South Dunes,** designated an Outstanding Natural Area by the Bureau of Land Management, are unvegetated, rising as high as 60 feet above the surrounding plains. Southwest winds, which formed them in the first place, are still urging them on at a rate of about a foot a year. Here, the dunes have the classic profile—a gentle windward slope and a steep leeward one.

South of the highway, an access road leads to the **North Dune Off-Road Vehicle Recreation Area❖,** which is open to recreation vehicles and camping. These northern dunes have been largely stabilized by a variety of vegetation including the shrubby shin oak and rabbitbrush. Cottonwood trees can grow in this desertlike place because the water table is near the surface.

A good time to visit is from late March to late April, when certain residents of the dunes north of Route 380 put on a remarkable show. These are prairie chickens, whose numbers, nationally, have declined along with the short-grass prairie. At dawn, the courting males, tail feathers spread into a fan, throat pouches full of air, take up positions in a circle called a lek, dance, and make astounding booming noises. One by one females enter the circle, choose a partner, and go off to mate. Anyone who has witnessed an Indian powwow where the dancers, extravagantly bedecked with feathers including a fanlike "bus-

---

LEFT: *Prickly pear cactus and yucca, common features of the Chihuahuan Desert, can be found on the slopes of such mountains as the Sacramentos. At about 4,000 feet desert plants give way to pinyon-juniper forest.*

ABOVE: *The giant desert hairy scorpion is a nocturnal predator up to five and a half inches long and itself prey of bats and owls; its very existence adds zest to any camper's night under the starry sky.*

tle," stomp and cock their heads in a birdlike manner will immediately recognize the powwow's origins in the prairie chicken lek. **New Mexico Department of Game and Fish Prairie Chicken Areas❖** also maintains other grounds, east and north near the towns of Milnesand, Crossroads, and Floyd, and inquiries to the department in Roswell will tell visitors the optimum sites. The town of Crossroads gained momentary fame in recent years when it was computed to be the safest place in the United States from the standpoint of earthquakes, tornadoes, and other natural disasters. They just don't happen there.

CARLSBAD CAVERNS

About 75 miles south of Roswell, both the Pecos River and Route 285 arrive in Carlsbad, and to the south and west of the city off Route 62-

ABOVE: *Less than three inches long, the hairy desert tarantula can live for two decades. It avoids daylight—and humans—whenever possible, and its venom is about as dangerous as that of the common bee.*

180 lies **Carlsbad Caverns National Park❖,** one of the most popular attractions in the state. For most people, it is sufficient to descend 750 feet by elevator and take a radio-guided tour through a labyrinth of passageways and huge chambers to the Big Room, a 14-acre space with ceilings as high as 200 feet—part of one of the world's largest fossil reefs. Called Capitan Reef, this massive ridge formed on the edge of an inland sea some 250 million years ago. After the sea dried up, the reef cracked—the joints determining where, much later, caves would form. The reef was then lifted along a fault, and groundwater seeped down along the joints, dissolving the limestone and forming underwater caverns. As the caverns dried out, acidic water continued to flow and drip and ooze, depositing calcium carbonate (limestone) and gypsum in a phantasmagoria of shapes. There are massive stalactites (hanging from

99

the ceiling) and stalagmites (growing from the ground); great curtains—some as high as 60 feet and some so thin light shines through them—called draperies (the result of flowing water); soda straws (from dripping water); stone lily pads; and mushroom-shaped rocks. There are helictites, spidery crystal-like formations with spines so thin they grow every which way by capillary action, not gravity. Some are so fragile a sneeze will break them. Above ground, between May and October at sundown, silent dark tornadoes of more than 500,000 bats issue forth from the caverns over a period of an hour, one of the more astounding sights in nature even though the bat population has declined from several million.

In all, there are more than 80 caves within the park, most of them protected, some open to experienced spelunkers. On all weekends and all summer days, visitors can take a guided tour of **Slaughter Canyon Cave,** full of wonders but explored only by lantern light (there are none of the lights, elevators, and eating places that one finds in the Big Room). Slaughter Canyon Cave lies in the mouth of Slaughter Canyon, which is the largest drainage in the section of the Guadalupe Mountains contained within Carlsbad Caverns National Park (the remaining mountains are in Lincoln National Forest and in Texas). Three miles up Middle Slaughter Canyon, through Chihuahuan Desert plants like sotol and cholla, and beyond into North Slaughter Canyon, is **Goat Cave,** an impressive (and little visited) place, a quarter-mile long and lit by a single "window."

The Guadalupe Mountains, also part of the great Capitan Reef, rise steeply as much as 4,000 feet above the surround. Cut by numerous canyons, such as Yucca, Double, and McKittrick, they provide splendid hiking areas through forests of pinyons, ponderosas, alligator junipers, and Gambel oaks. In October, the canyons are radiant with autumn's last fling.

Seventy miles west of Carlsbad Caverns National Park on Route 137 is **Sitting Bull Falls❖,** where water drops 130 feet—the largest falls in the state—depositing a huge bluff of travertine that looms up over a picnic

ABOVE: *The four-inch-long Mexican free-tailed bat is Carlsbad Caverns' most populous denizen. At approximately 100 million, they are one of the most numerous mammals in North America.*

LEFT: *Pictured on an early postcard, one of the original explorers of Carlsbad Caverns, Jim White, stands near the point where the route from the Big Room to the Lower Cave first gave a clue to the caverns' enormous extent.*

101

ground. A trail leads up to the top of the falls and back along a many-pooled stream to Sitting Bull Springs. Less strenuous is the Walnut Canyon loop drive, which starts at the park's visitor center and runs for about nine miles through desert and canyon country.

A must for the naturalist is **Rattlesnake Springs❖,** an 80-acre detached unit of Carlsbad Caverns, joined by a 13.5-acre desert oasis preserved by the Nature Conservancy. The Park Service maintains an adjacent picnic ground, a good vantage point to look at the sedges and cattails that flourish in a marsh and the large cottonwoods that bespeak the riparian area. Rare birds such as Bell's vireo and the varied bunting visit here, and it is a prime nesting spot for turkey vultures. The springs are popular with visitors interested in reptiles and amphibians because the area is home to two state-listed "herps": the Pecos western ribbon snake and the eastern barking frog. In addition, it has the only known colony of the Texas emperor butterfly, too rare to appear in standard guidebooks. Here in this lush oasis it is difficult to recall, even imagine, the arid heat, the hot lava beds, and the dust of the Jornada del Muerto.

RIGHT: *The emergence at dusk of hundreds of thousands of Mexican free-tailed bats led explorers to Carlsbad Caverns. Each morning at sunrise, the bats plummet from about 1,000 feet up at 25 miles an hour straight down into the entrance.*

THE APACHERIA: SOUTHWESTERN NEW MEXICO

To claim the southwestern quarter of New Mexico as "the Apacheria" is, of course, to overlook the fact that Mescalero Apache roamed (and controlled) most of southeastern New Mexico—the Jicarillos the northeast, and the Navajo (of Apache lineage) much of the northwest. In the southwestern part of the state the group loosely known as the Chiricahua also held sway (as well as in a part of adjacent Arizona). And here the last of the Chiricahua became the final free-roaming Indians on the continent to surrender to the onslaught of United States hegemony. Never numbering more than a thousand, if that, the Chiricahua bands owed their success in forestalling this fate to their nearly perfect adaptation to life in the rugged mountains and dry basins of the region.

Living in small bands of near relatives, they were seminomadic, moving up and down the slopes with the season like deer and bears and other predators. They hunted, gathered, planted a bit of corn in season, raided for horses, and resented with a steadfast fury any interference with their lives. As a result, they were among the fiercest guerrilla fighters in human history, withstanding intrusions by Spanish, Mexicans, and Anglos—and other Indians—for more than 200 years.

LEFT: *Born near Gila National Monument in what many consider the state's grandest wilderness region, the west fork of the Gila River begins its long journey to the Colorado River in western Arizona.*

They knew every tiny water source in this arid land; they could melt into the crags, even (it is said) disappear behind a few blades of grass in the desert. No one has learned better how to live in such an unforgiving, though for them all-giving, place.

Finally, mining and cattle interests became too great, and the Apache were eventually put down, Geronimo and 20-odd followers surrendering for the last time in 1886 in Skeleton Canyon, just inside the New Mexico border in the Peloncillo Mountains. They capitulated only after several years of being chased by one quarter of the entire U.S. Army. A few mostly lone stragglers remained at large, even into this century. One of them, a former tracker and scout for the cavalry who came to be called the Apache Kid, managed to make a feral living in the region until 1907.

To visit the natural areas of this part of New Mexico, even the most remote and least trammeled, is to step where these great warriors once hunted, prayed to their gods, lived by their beliefs, and struck terror into the souls of their enemies.

It remains a difficult and uncompromising land. In the northern part, vulcanism has created a great jumble of mountain ranges, which separate the Colorado Plateau from the classic basin and range country to the south. North-south ranges have heaved up and worn down, their detritus making flat and usually enclosed basins from which the little water that arrives has no place to go and simply evaporates. The result is alkaline flats called playas. An area sufficient to house four New Jerseys, the Apacheria supports only about 75,000 people, most of whom are located in five small "cities." Here is some of the least traveled backcountry in the state, vast amounts of open ground. But even the least-promising land may prove recreational: Near Lordsburg, barren and windblown flats, once an enormous lake, serve again as a "lake," providing a substrate for the wheels and multicolored sails of windracers.

SOUTH OF SOCORRO, WEST OF THE RIO GRANDE

On the crest south of Blue Mountain in the **San Mateo Mountains,** a marker acknowledges the death of the Apache Kid. Although no one

---

OVERLEAF: *Rocky Mountain iris, painted in hues of violet, and the new sun welcome the intrepid hiker into the San Mateo Mountains, a rugged, little-trammeled wilderness area south of the city of Socorro.*

APACHERIA

25 — 0 — 25 Miles
25 — 0 — 25 Kilometers

ARIZONA

Albuquerque

Sandia Mtns

40
25
Belen
60
Manzano Mtns

117
36
Quemado
60
32

CIBOLA
NATIONAL
Datil
12
FOR
WATER CANYON CAMPGRD
Socorro
380
San Antonio

APACHE NATIONAL FOREST
180
12

Mt Withington 10115
60
BEAR TRAP CAMPGROUND
WITHINGTON WILDERNESS

San Mateo Mtns

APACHE KID WILDERNESS

GILA
CONTINENTAL DIVIDE
52
SPRINGTIME CAMPGROUND

WHITE
SANDS
MISSILE
RANGE

Jornado del Muerto

Tularosa Valley

Mogollon Mountains

NATIONAL
GILA WILDERNESS
Lightfoot Hot Springs

GILA CLIFF DWELLINGS NAT MON

180
15
FOREST
152
Elephant Butte Reservoir
Truth or Consequences

San Andres Mtns

54

Alamogordo

Mangas Springs

Gila River
Lower Box
GILA NAT FOR
Silver City
61
City of Rocks SP
Cookes Peak 8408

25

SAN ANDRES NATIONAL WILDLIFE REFUGE

WHITE SANDS NATIONAL MONUMENT

70
WHITE SANDS MISSILE RANGE
Baylor Pass
54

CONTINENTAL DIVIDE
90
180
Deming
Rio

70
Las Cruces
Organ Mtns

CHIHUAHUA
70
80
10
ROCK HOUND STATE PARK
Florida Mtns
10
AGUIRRE SPRINGS RECREATION AREA
DRIPPING SPRINGS NATURAL AREA

9
Animas

81

Peloncillo Mtns

DESERT

TEXAS
El Paso

CORONADO NATIONAL FOREST
Guadelupe Canyon
Antelope Wells

MEXICO

10

knows for sure, he might well have lived and died in these mountains, for they provide the kind of fastness where such a man could have eluded the rest of the world for almost 20 years. The San Mateos are a 32-mile-long range, volcanic in origin, southwest of Socorro off Interstate 25. They lie between the Rio Grande Valley and, to the west, the plains of San Augustin, a lowland area surrounded by mountains and home of the Very Large Array. These stark white dishes form a grand and mysterious-looking ring of brave, white radio telescopes where a consortium of astronomers look for the likes of pulsars.

On the east, the ragged red slabs of the San Mateos, part of the far-flung holdings of the **Cibola National Forest❖,** rise steeply in vertiginous crags up to 4,000 feet above the valley floor. To the west they slope more gently (here used relatively). Logging has succeeded only around the gentler perimeter, and prospectors found little in the interior. It has been said that even few New Mexico natives know of this rugged place and the gem it contains in its interior—the **Apache Kid Wilderness,** a place recommended only to those with good backcountry skills.

Most of the visitors who hike into this region leave from **Springtime Campground,** off Route 225 in the southern part of the wilderness, to take the 13-mile Apache Kid trail up the crest to Blue Mountain and beyond. Along this pathway, and some 70 miles of side trails, are 7,000-foot-high meadows with grasses and wildflowers up to the knee, bushy Apache pines, ponderosas, and primeval stands of Douglas fir. These upper realms have been largely untouched for centuries, and in this old growth dwell a few spotted owls. Hikers may be barked at by tassel-eared squirrels and Gila woodpeckers. Wildlife typical of the southwestern mountains abounds—elk, mule and white-tailed deer, mountain lions, black bears, eagles, a variety of hawks, jays, Merriam's turkeys, and harlequin quail—and in autumn the highlands, which exceed 10,000 feet, are aflame with the gold of aspens.

From many peaks and trails in the wilderness, vistas extend across Elephant Butte Reservoir to the Sacramentos 75 miles east and 40 miles southwest to the Gila Mountains. To the north lies the smaller (19,000-acre) **Withington Wilderness,** basically more of the same but crossed by far fewer trails: It is probably the least-frequented wilderness area in the state. **Beartrap Campground,** reached via Route 168 south from Route 60 out of Magdalena, provides access, as do several unimproved forest roads that come within a few miles of 10,115-foot Mount Withington. One indefatigable explorer of New Mexico's mountains has said that this is the place to escape "in-laws and the IRS."

Incidentally, for those to whom the San Mateos seem a bit strenuous, local birders highly recommend a stay at **Water Canyon Campground** in the Magdalena Mountains just outside Socorro off Route 60. Located in a riparian woodland of narrowleaf cottonwoods, alders, and willows, two gentle strolls and one mildly aerobic hike up a forest road offer a rich bird fauna including gray, solitary, Hutton's, and warbling vireos; red-faced warblers; and many jays and woodpeckers.

By any standard, one of the most beautiful drives in the state is Route 152 (running west from Interstate 25 south of Truth or Consequences—a town originally called Hot Springs and renamed for the old radio show for purposes best known to the chamber of commerce), through the charming little eyeblink town of Hillsboro and up into the **Gila National Forest❖.** The road switchbacks up some 3,000 feet in the space of ten miles, through the classic vegetation zones up to about 8,000 feet at Emory Pass. Indeed, any passable road into this forest deserves the label "scenic drive," and several lead into this largest of the state's national forests—almost 3.3 million acres. Some say that if a visitor to New Mexico can go but one place to hike and wander, this is it, though in fact to explore it all would take a lifetime.

ABOVE: *In 1916 American artist Louis Agassiz Fuertes, considered one of the greatest portraitists in ornithology, painted this watercolor of a hybrid quail.*

Many people are drawn to the **Gila Cliff Dwellings National Monument❖,** which is about 45 miles—and a beautiful two-hour drive—north of Silver City on Route 15. A visitor center serves both the monument and the forest, and a half-mile trail leads to the cliffs. Percolating water has eroded weak spots in the rock, mostly a conglomerate of pebbles and cobbles in a calcium carbonate matrix, creat-

111

ABOVE: *Silent ruins in the Gila Cliff Dwellings National Monument whisper about the people, members of what is called the Mimbres Culture, who built there in about A.D. 1200 and then vanished into history.*

ing alcoves in the canyon walls. Some 700 years ago, prehistoric people of the culture we call Mimbres, which arose from the Mogollon, built stone villages in the shelter of these caves, only to leave about two centuries later, probably run off by the newly arrived Apache.

Remote as it is, this spot is the confluence of many things. The cliffs themselves are part of an uplifted fault block that extends from the basin and range lands to the south. The whole region is volcanic in origin, and Vulcan's forge is still to be experienced in the numerous hot springs that bubble up. Some have been commercialized and others, such as **Lightfoot Hot Springs,** a half-mile up the middle fork of the Gila River from the visitor center, simply await the avid bather who wishes to take the waters enjoyed certainly by Apache and probably by their Mimbres and Mogollon predecessors. Here and there the groundwater, heated by hot rocks below, has leached out of the pores of Mother Earth, producing spots of yellow clay just like those that give Yellowstone National Park its name.

This enormous forest has everything one might seek in a national forest except tundra (its highest peaks are 10,000-footers) and grizzly bears and wolves (wiped out long ago by such heroes as the famed mountain man Ben Lilly). But it encompasses three major wilderness areas, including the first one ever to receive such a designation with a capital W.

The **Gila Wilderness,** more than a half-million acres, was established in 1924, largely through the advocacy of Aldo Leopold, a forest ranger who would become, through such writings as *Sand County*

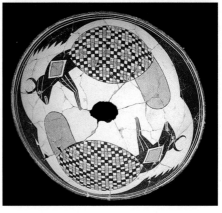

ABOVE: *Master potters, the Mimbres people adorned their distinctive black-on-white pots, made from coils of clay, with whimsical animals, such as the decorative bat (top) and a pair of horned insects (bottom). The pots often accompanied the dead in their graves.*

OVERLEAF: *Lit by the late sun, Snake Ridge and the distant Mogollon Mountains preside over Whitewater Creek in the Gila Wilderness, one of three such areas designated in the Gila National Forest, including the nation's first, the Aldo Leopold Wilderness.*

Almanac, America's preeminent guru of land ethics. It includes the Mogollon Mountains and some of it is on the Colorado Plateau, making it a place of unusual variety of life-forms in the Southwest and also the forest's most popular backpacking and hiking area. The **Aldo Leopold Wilderness** comprises most of the Black Range, in the eastern part of the forest—some 20,000 acres of rugged mountains and canyons. None of these wilderness areas are overrun, but the least frequented is the Blue Range Wilderness, about 30,000 acres that lie northwest of Silver City—a steep, secluded place straddling the Mogollon Rim. A good wilderness map will help visitors navigate these areas.

The general area of the visitor center includes yet another important feature of Gila country: Here three forks join to form the **Gila River,** which eventually crosses the state of Arizona and joins up with the Colorado. A pleasant hiking trail begins at the cliff dwellings parking lot and leads along the West Fork through ponderosas (which can live at such a low elevation because of unusual wetness of the surrounding mountains), past some beaver dams into the wilderness, and to a spectacular rocky chasm with a cliff dwelling improbably high up on the canyon wall.

A hiking trail parallels the first 30 miles of the Gila River (from where it crosses Route 15), and all the way to the town of Gila, it passes through magnificent canyons. For the first seven or so miles it is narrow and has few rapids; thereafter it is nearly incessant class II and III rapids with a good deal of portaging. South of the town of Gila on Route 180, about 13 miles outside Silver City, is **Mangas Springs.** There a blacktop road leads down to a marsh that serves as a migratory bird "trap," and one may find black-throated blue and blackpoll warblers among the numerous songbirds, not to mention (with luck) a black hawk.

Below the town of Red Rock, the river enters the **Lower Box❖,** managed by the Bureau of Land Management. Nearly vertical canyon walls sometimes reach 600 feet and the vegetation along the banks is unusually lush (in contrast to the desertlands above) with Arizona sycamores and walnuts, as well as cottonwoods and willows. Thanks to this growth, the wildlife is also unusually dense: The canyon swarms with great concentrations of more than a hundred breeding species of birds, as well as many more avian visitors throughout the year, and mammals, reptiles, and amphibians abound. From Red Rock to Virden

ABOVE: *Beginning at about 7,000 feet elevation, stately ponderosa pines dominate forests such as those in Gallinas Canyon in the Black Range, part of Gila National Forest's more than 3 million acres.*

on the Arizona border are 20 miles of class I and II rapids, and the canyon and its many side canyons can be hiked.

If, instead of drifting prematurely into Arizona, one heads south and east of Silver City into the basin and range country, **City of Rocks State Park❖** provides a bizarre sight and a good campground. Located off Route 180 on Route 61, its 680 acres hold the oddly eroded remains of a field of volcanic tuff, rock formed from an ashflow. Well worth the detour, this is an otherworldly city of great lumpy buildings, vaguely like an early stab at Stonehenge. Beyond to the southeast, in stunning isolation, **Cookes Peak❖** looms 3,000 feet above the surrounding desert, a granite crag that reminds some climbers of the Matterhorn. Once used as a lookout by the Apache and now part of the holdings of the Bureau of Land Management, the peak is a strenuous five-and-a-half-mile climb. The result of a huge intrusion through sedimentary rocks now mostly worn

117

ABOVE: *Snakeweed blooming bright yellow, prickly pear cactus, and balls of spiky sotol bedeck the eastern slopes of the rugged and challenging Organ Mountains in Aguirre Springs Recreation Area.*

away, Cookes Peak marks the western edge of the Rio Grande Rift.

South and east of Deming, the **Florida Mountains❖** rise like the silhouette of a battleship. Hiking is excellent in this Bureau of Land Management range, named for the dense flora the Spanish found there. In the foothills, off Interstate 10, is a place where the old adage—take only what you came with—is expressly contradicted. This is **Rock Hound State Park❖,** where one is encouraged to poke around in the dust for such goodies as perlites, carnelians, amethysts, spherelites, geodes, and thunder eggs. Once the place has been picked clean, the state parks people simply blade it down to another treasure-laden layer.

East to Las Cruces (on the other side of the Rio Grande), the skyline is dominated by the great pinnacles and spires of the **Organ Mountains❖.** Once known to the Spanish as La Sierra de la Soledad (Mountains of Solitude), they remain aloof even though they are now cheek-by-jowl with a medium-sized city. The Organs are a 20-mile ridge with San Augustin Peak on the north end and Rattlesnake Ridge to the south. In

118

between lies a batholith, a huge, faulted igneous body of pinkish quartz monzonite carved into organ-pipe–like needles. The range rises some 5,000 feet above the surround, and its steep spires attract technical climbers. Access on both the west and east sides of the mountains is from Route 70, and campgrounds and hiking trails laid out by the Bureau of Land Management invite visitors. Many of the trails run through cactus, thornbush, and yucca, which makes life a bit difficult, as does a good deal of loose rock. Climbers are advised to clap their hands frequently to make the abundant rattlesnakes rattle so that they may be avoided.

These hazards notwithstanding, the Organs are a relatively popular draw (areas on the west side have been set aside for off-road vehicle use), and there are numerous places, particularly in the south, where only a few human flies on the spires above break the solitude. An easy day hike is from a trailhead about six miles past **Aguirre Springs Recreation Area❖** two miles up to Baylor Pass. A short way beyond that trailhead is another, the Pine Tree Trail, a fairly simple hike to the base of the needles and spires among huge alligator junipers with spectacular views north as far as Sierra Blanca. One of the treasures of the Organ Mountains is the **Dripping Springs Natural Area❖,** administered by the BLM in cooperation with the Nature Conservancy. The 2,850-acre natural area of volcanic cliffs, sheer canyons, and permanent water sources is nestled at the base of the mountains and on the edge of the Chihuahuan Desert. It is reached by driving east on Las Cruces' University Avenue—a ten-mile stretch of gravel road. The road ends at the A. B. Cox Visitor Center, where hikers register for the trail to Dripping Springs. The preserve's naturally occurring water sources make for a rich and varied habitat, home for such plants as velvet ash, Arizona white oak, netleaf hackberry, and the rare Organ Mountain evening primrose. Prairie falcons soar overhead, canyon wrens carry on in the canyons, as they should, and other songbirds, including the black-chinned sparrow, abound.

THE BOOTHEEL

In the southwestern corner of New Mexico a rectangle of land dips south into Mexico, and here is a world apart. One of the least populated parts of a little-populated region, it consists mostly of private ranch-

land and partly forested north-south–running mountain chains—the Hatchets, the Animas, the Peloncillos. The world stretches away in silence to these saw-toothed mountains, and to the vast empty reaches of Mexico. Antelope Wells, located at mile 0 on Route 81, is the most re-mote and least trafficked crossing along the entire Mexico–U.S. border—rarely do more than ten cars a day pass through. Not far from this crossing Black Jack Pershing amassed his troops in 1916 to punish Pancho Villa for making the first, and last, invasion of the United States since 1812.

A sizable fraction of the bootheel is the fabled **Gray Ranch,** which in 1990 be-came the largest single private conservation purchase in United States history. The Nature Conservancy took command of 502 square miles, an area almost exactly half of the state of Rhode Island. The ranch, dot-ted with at least 13 old ruins from the Mesa Verde culture, is bisected by the Animas Mountains, the southern terminus of the United States portion of the Continental Divide. The western basin is dominated by what was not so long ago a lake but is now a largely undergrazed pasture of 44,000 acres—a pasture big enough to hold three Manhattan Islands—with a few fences, windmills, and camps. To call it a sea of grass is to understate the matter, and its beauty lies beyond mere words when the goldeneye blooms in the autumn and turns virtually the entire 44,000 acres a bright yellow.

What the conservancy sought to pre-serve (as does the private Animas Founda-tion that has since bought the property) is an entire landscape, one of the few such

In an undergrazed grassland the size of three Manhattans, a clump of bear grass (left) and a soap tree yucca (above) hold their own with-in sight of the Animas Moun-tains on the renowned Gray Ranch, a private conserva-tion holding and working cattle ranch in New Mexico's remote southern bootheel.

121

areas anywhere in the West that, miraculously, was never severely overgrazed. Instead, its grasslands look Pleistocene in their pure lushness and it would not, somehow, be surprising to see a mastodon herd wandering past. The ranch contains about 30 endangered species of animals and a like number of endangered plants in some 60 distinct plant associations, many to be found on the slopes and in the canyons of the Animas chain. In all, nearly 300 species of vertebrates dwell on Gray Ranch, and there has been talk of transplanting some California condors to the crags of the Animas Mountains. Here the only United States populations of many Mexican species are found, such as the white-sided jackrabbit and the Mexican checkerspot, a red, white, and black butterfly, one of 130 butterfly species on the place.

Among the severely endangered species found on the ranch are the Emory oak, the Animas Peak woodsnail, the Mexican and Sanborn's long-nosed bats, the lowland leopard frog, Baird's sparrow, and the Chiricahua Mountain larkspur, as well as several endangered plant communities. A few remaining members of a subspecies of ridge-nosed rattlesnakes are highly prized. There are numerous pronghorns and deer roaming the grasslands and foothills; collared peccaries (locally called javelinas) bustle around at dusk; and coyotes yip and howl through the night.

Long closed as private land, the ranch has become a mecca for scientific censusing and will no doubt yield new ecological insights into a variety of habitats that are elsewhere less undisturbed. The new owner has yet to announce exact plans for this astounding holding, but access by the public, if there is to be any at all, will almost surely be on a limited reservation basis.

Some of the unusual species living on Gray Ranch can be found in the **Peloncillo Mountains,** which form (loosely) the western extreme of the ranch. Part of the **Coronado National Forest❖,** these volcanic mountains straddle the New Mexico–Arizona border and rise to some 6,500 feet, lower by about 2,000 feet than the Animas chain; they are exceedingly remote and rarely visited. They are mostly low, rounded hills with grass, oak, and pinyon-juniper forest, cut by

LEFT: *Sycamore trees line a dry wash in Guadalupe Canyon athwart the New Mexico–Arizona border, providing nesting sites for a rainbow of birds and unparalleled viewing opportunities for birders.*

canyons running in all directions.

One can reach the Peloncillos by driving 30 miles south of the town of Animas on Route 338, then turning west at the junction toward Douglas, Arizona, on Forest Road 63. Two miles into the Coronado Forest, a left fork leads up a bank to a flat area. A two-and-a-half-mile hike up **Clanton Draw** (named for the Clanton brothers, outlaws who lost at the OK Corral) leads through stands of Chiricahua pines to Blackwater Hole, a relatively constant water source.

These mountains are famous among birders (Strickland's wood-pecker appears here, among others), but *the* place for birds in New Mexico is in **Guadalupe Canyon❖,** in the southernmost part of the Peloncillos on the Mexican border. It is a holding of the Bureau of Land Management, which has named it an Outstanding Natural Area. To get there, continue past the fork on Forest Road 63 to a picnic area, from which the entrance to Guadalupe Canyon (in Arizona) is about 24 miles away. The canyon, not very deep, is wooded with cotton-woods, sycamores, and Arizona white oaks, and is one of the few places in the United States where one can see the fan-tailed warbler and the elegant (formerly coppery-tailed) trogon, one of the Mexican species whose ranges slip over slightly into the United States. The even rarer eared trogon has been reported here, and those good at night birding might spot a buff-collared nightjar. More likely one may hear this bird's call, more than likely a mockingbird mimicking the nightjar. Lucifer and Costa's hummingbirds appear here along with many others of their tribe, and some unusual flycatchers also number among the approximately 160 birds found in the canyon.

The canyon lies athwart the state border, which is about three miles in from the canyon entrance. Preoccupied birders may not know at any given moment whether they are in New Mexico or Arizona, and the birds, of course, make no such distinction. Guadalupe Canyon, with its teeming, jewel-like birdlife, one of the wonders of the Southwest, thus serves as an appropriate transition from the Land of Enchantment into the southern reaches of the Grand Canyon State.

RIGHT: *A male elegant trogon perches regally on a branch. Related to the legendary quetzal of the Mayans, this trogon is a must-see Mexican species for any serious birder visiting the Southwest.*

ARIZONA

PART TWO

A R I Z O N A

I

f there is an elegiac, saffron essence to New Mexico, arising from the peculiar quality of the light and perhaps the prevalence of its ancient Spanish heritage, Arizona can be characterized as exuberant, more given to primary colors than earth tones. Arizona seems recently discovered, brand-new every day, while New Mexico has been there, little changed, forever.

Generalizations, of course, rarely hold up to complete scrutiny: In northeastern Arizona, brooding on the edge of three yellow sandstone mesas, are the ancient habitations of the Hopi, one of whose towns, Oraibi, is said to be the oldest continuously inhabited place on the continent (though New Mexico's Acoma pueblo makes the same claim). But for the most part, non-Indian history in Arizona *is* of more recent origin. Except for a few outposts like Tucson, the Spanish presence was slight, thanks largely (again) to the Apache, whose implacable presence split the Spanish incursions into two prongs—up the Rio Grande and into California—just as the Rio Grande Rift split the southern tail of the Rocky Mountains.

A sizable Anglo presence was felt statewide (or territory-wide, to be precise) only well into the nineteenth century. A visitor to Tucson today will quickly sense, under its layers of twentieth-century urban technology and sophistication, the nearly heedless but thoroughly exciting bustle of a frontier town. The town fathers fret that there may not be, exactly, a "Tucson style" in the sense that there is a "Santa Fe style."

If there is an Arizona style, it has something to do with superlatives. It is after all the Grand Canyon State, properly proud of one of the seven wonders of the world within its borders. We associate su-

---

PRECEDING PAGES: *Under a lowering sky, the sun sets majestically beyond the Grand Canyon, the mightiest gash in the planet's surface, seen here from the tip of the South Rim's glowing Yaki Point.*

perlatives with Texas, but Arizonans will have none of that. Although, at about 113,000 square miles, Arizona is a fraction smaller than New Mexico and not even half the size of Texas, Arizonans like to explain "real" size to the swaggering folk of the Lone Star State. If, they say, you could grasp Arizona firmly by its eastern and western borders and pop it out flat, like most of Texas, its deep canyons and unending mountains would create a space so large that you could throw all of Texas into one corner and lose it altogether.

That image is the key to understanding the natural places of Arizona: Besides vistas that stretch the eyes, it has nooks and crannies and verticality, some places spectacularly grand, some grandly intimate. It is home to the world's greatest canyon, but also to uncounted thousands of other canyons. Within its borders are 193 distinct mountain *ranges,* which come in five different flavors, and four major desert types adorn the land. Although it is far more populated than its neighbor (it has about 3.5 million inhabitants to New Mexico's 1.5 million), there are large empty expanses in Arizona. Virtually no one goes to the southern desert in the summer heat, not even the late writer Edward Abbey, that redneck philosopher of desert purity and of fine anarchy in general.

Like King Canute and the oceans, Abbey railed against the human junking of what he had found to be pristine; he loved it still, and in a novel, *The Monkey Wrench Gang,* he imagined how to throw a spanner in the engine of civilization. He called Tucson "the Blob" and featured Phoenix in a doomsday novel. Growling boisterously till the end, he extolled the glory of the rocks and the light and the land and the desert tortoises.

There would seem to be a bit of Ed Abbey—not necessarily his studied misanthropy but his nearly feral love of the Arizona outdoors—in most Arizonans. Although the effect of environment on character is hard to prove, in Arizona it has to have something to do with giant cacti, dust, and erosion, with flash floods and heat mirages, with the astonishing inventiveness, the capacity to surprise, the multicolored, carefree, liberating, sense-altering grandness of the land itself.

OVERLEAF: *In his 1855 painting* The Chain of Spires Along the Gila River, *artist John Mix Stanley accurately recorded a desert realm and its denizens through the romantic and kindly eyes of the Hudson River School.*

CHAPTER FIVE

BASIN AND RANGE: SOUTHERN ARIZONA

Mountain range after gaunt mountain range stretches across the land like blue rows of carnivorous teeth, separated by broad flat plains, or basins, a region that sweeps across Arizona from New Mexico to California and up to the Utah border. This is the desert for which Arizona is so noted—uncomfortably, even dangerously hot in the summer months. It is in fact four deserts. The Chihuahuan Desert slips across the New Mexico border a few miles and soon becomes the Sonoran. Across the state, in the west-central area, the Mojave Desert leaks over from California, and in the northwestern corner is the southern fringe of the Great Basin Desert, which stretches all the way to southern Idaho and Oregon.

Dust devils swirl up from time to time in these lands, and enormous dust storms may darken the sky, usually followed by brown clouds and heavy rains. But for the most part there is a great stillness here, a fine silence under bright heavens. Yet as geologists reckon time, this basin and range province has been the most active, even mobile, region in Arizona. During the last 75 million years, underlying tectonic plates have pushed and pulled apart, creating huge mountain ridges running north-south or northeast-southwest. And these have

LEFT: *In prickly diversity, barrel, cholla, and, in the distance, organ-pipe cacti fill the eye at Organ Pipe Cactus National Monument, with the saw-toothed Ajo Mountains rising on the distant horizon.*

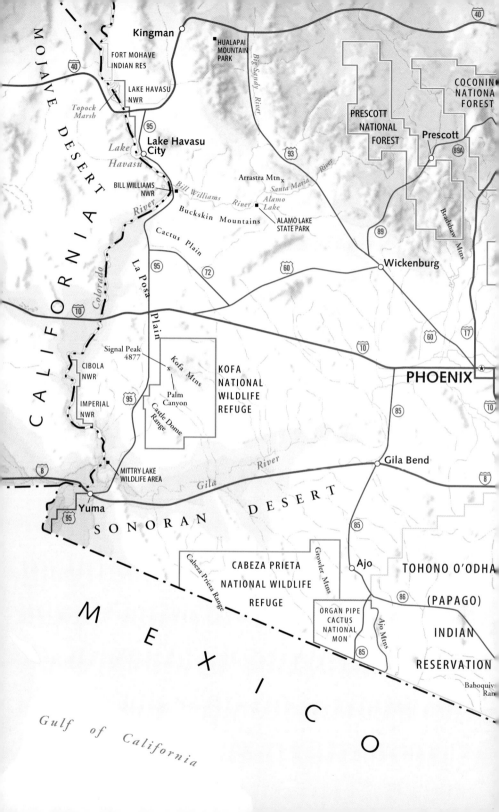

been worn down by water and dust-laden wind: Great aprons of sand and gravel called alluvial fans indicate the former or occasional presence of a rushing stream after heavy rainfalls. Many alluvial fans have coalesced into *bajadas* that ring the mountain range and extend out into the basin. The basins between ranges can contain up to thousands of feet of valley fill, much of it salty. Left behind when the wind urges the finer grains of sand elsewhere is a densely packed layer of pebbles—desert pavement. These pebbles and the cliffs of the mountains are often found covered with desert varnish—an accumulation of iron and manganese derived from the dust itself. Although the landscape seems to bespeak a great and brooding antiquity, its land*forms* are among the state's most recent.

At various times, the region has hosted a large sea, and it is only recently a desert. In the time of the glaciers 10,000 to 20,000 years ago, this was a cooler place, lusher, and the remnants of these cooler times are to be found in its "sky islands." These areas were formed as the glaciers retreated in the north and the lowlands began to dry out and heat up. Relics of those Pleistocene times—Engelmann spruce, for example—remained on top of the mountains. On these islands in the desert, creatures like the red squirrel have gone about their affairs in isolation from others of their kind, becoming distinct subspecies, or even new species known nowhere else.

Here also, in the southern part of the state, many northern and Mexican species reach the limits of their ranges, coexisting in a fine cosmopolitan blend. This picture is different from the one "desert" typically brings to mind. It is a breathtaking mosaic of landforms and life zones, one of the most biologically diverse regions in the country. And no place in the region is more diverse than the Chiricahua Mountains, a 500-square-mile range that is one of 11 separate ranges within the far-flung Coronado National Forest. So great a jumble of heavily eroded peaks, canyons, and cliffs are these mountains that not until the 1960s were geologists able to pin down the exact location of the caldera that resulted when 25 million years ago, violent volcanic

RIGHT: *Eroded volcanic remnants, a veritable army of pinnacles, steeples, and hoodoos, stand silent sentry duty in Chiricahua National Monument, seen here from Sugarloaf Mountain at day's end.*

ABOVE: *Easily mistaken by both humans and its predators for a dangerous coral snake, the tricolored Sonora mountain kingsnake conserves its venom for hunting its own prey, lizards and rodents.*

action covered the area with thousands of feet of rhyolite rock, the foundation of the Chiricahuas.

THE SOUTHEAST

When one plummets west from New Mexico through the pass on Route 9 in the Peloncillo Mountains, the Chiricahuas appear to soar straight up, abrupt and forbidding, a fortress of crags, spires, pinnacles, and battlements that served well as an Apache stronghold. Today, the hamlet of Portal sits at the gateway to **Cave Creek Canyon❖.** Here two peaks rise several thousand precipitous feet above the creek, and just upstream looms the monolith Cathedral Rock—a vista often called Arizona's Yosemite. Beyond the peaks, the south and main forks of Cave Creek

ABOVE RIGHT: *Among the least aggressive of the dozen western rattlers, the black-tailed rattlesnake with its light-centered crossbands frequents mountainous, rocky places and is abroad both night and day.*

meet. Up the narrow canyon of the **South Fork,** bizarre rock formations and towering red-orange cliffs (tinted green with lichens) are pocked with wind caves. The **Main Fork** widens into the remains of the caldera and a sweeping pine forest where Hudsonian trees in the upper peaks are nearly 10,000 feet high. Abundant trails lead up through forests containing Arizona pines, alligator junipers, then pine-oak woods with Chiricahua and Apache pines (the latter reaching its northern limit here), and eventually Engelmann spruces on the peaks.

Jaguarundis (small, unspotted jaguars) occur only here and in extreme southern Texas, and jaguars have been seen here as well. Porcupines go no farther south, coatis (grayish-brown mammals similar to raccoons) no farther north, and the Apache fox squirrel is known only here. The mountains are prowled by bobcats, mountain lions, and bears, and there are various species of endangered bats (important pollinators of century plants), 4 species of skunks, an astounding 30 species of snakes including 6 kinds of rattlers, and 25,000 species of insects. More is known of this sky island than any other, thanks to the presence for the past three decades of the American Museum of Natural History's Southwestern Research Station above Portal, which has more Ph.D.'s per capita than anywhere else in the United States.

Despite these riches, the main draw is the birds. Cave Creek Canyon is the most reliable place to see such southern species as the elegant trogon, even the eared trogon some years, the Mexican chickadee, and various unusual hummingbirds. Of 34 diurnal raptors on the continent, 24 occur here, as well as dozens of owls. And up the Main Fork, thick-billed parrots were recently reintroduced to the wild after some 50 years. In all, more than 330 bird species have been recorded in this drainage, including a greater diversity of breeding land birds than any other place in the country. Not surprisingly, birders make the most of the area and its campgrounds, especially in spring and early fall, but it is also host to picnickers, hikers, campers, even spelunkers who, after obtaining a key from the Forest Service in Douglas, Arizona, can explore the marvels of **Crystal Cave,** located west of Round Mountain.

In the northwestern corner of these mountains, a 12,000-acre area was set aside in 1924 as **Chiricahua National Monument❖.** Here one walks *down* through various life zones, for this is ridge and canyon country. On the high, arid, windswept ridges are clusters of low, leathery-leaved oaks and manzanitas—including chaparral, the dwarf evergreen oak. In the canyons the vegetation changes 100 feet down to tall shaded forests of mixed conifers—including Arizona cypress and the startlingly red-branched madrone, a deciduous tree. To such zones, a few permanent streams such as Rhyolite Creek add riparian habitat.

Here and there one notices what seems a cluster of yellow pincushions—the Cochise rock daisy, which grows only in the monument.

RIGHT: *Like a cosmic chess set, the eroded rhyolite columns near Echo Canyon catch the sun at Heart of Rocks in Chiricahua National Monument.*
OVERLEAF: *A grotto carved from the volcanic rock by wind and water in Chiricahua National Monument beckons one into a fairy-tale world.*

One might spy a yellow-and-brown-striped lizard, the Chihuahua spotted whiptail, one of 13 lizard species that come in but one flavor: female. They reproduce via unfertilized eggs—that is, they are clones. Everywhere lichens adhere to the rocks, trees, and fallen logs. As many as 30 lichen species have been found on a single species of oak. Harmless to trees, lichens do play a role in eroding rock, and this became a national monument because of the rocks.

After the volcanic period, huge chunks of dun-colored rhyolite were heaved upward, layered as the result of multiple eruptions. Immediately the tools of erosion went to work on the cracks, leaving behind phalanx after phalanx of pinnacles, 100-foot-high columns, steeples, and hoodoos (fantastic stone shapes, sometimes columns with a large rock balanced on top). Entire hillsides seem alive with these silent sentinels. In Heart of Rocks, a huge array was seen as chesspieces huddled together at one end of a chessboard, and some arrays have been compared to the giant stone heads of Easter Island. Heaven only knows what images they elicited from the Indians who lived here.

A few miles west of Willcox on I-10, the land stretching to the south is featureless, dead white. This is the **Willcox Playa❖,** the remnant of a once great lake that filled most of Sulphur Springs Valley; the old shores are visible as dunes near Willcox. Throughout most of the basin and range region, the basins filled up with so much detritus from the surrounding mountains that streams eventually were able to flow out into other basins. Not here; even though there is about 2,000 feet of valley fill under the playa, there remains no drainage out of the valley. The sporadic rains that fall, sometimes in torrents, still drain into this lowest point. The playa is so flat that a quarter-inch of standing water will stretch for miles. As the water evaporates, it adds another thin alkaline layer to the glaring white crust of carbonates, a process that has been going on since prehistoric times.

Most of the playa is a U.S. Army reserve bombing range, but the Bureau of Land Management has designated some 2,500 acres in the northwest as a National Natural Landmark. And the Arizona Game and

LEFT: *Snow softens the sharp edges of Chiricahua's Echo Canyon; in the narrow seams and crannies of its rock ledges, tenacious spiny yuccas and hardy Mexican pinyon eke out their meager livings.*

ABOVE: *Ears up, a mule deer stands alert by a thorny backlit ocotillo. Today the chief hunters of these deer are human; the feline ones with whom it evolved (mainly mountain lions) are now rarely seen.*

Fish Department manages about 500 acres on the eastern edge of the playa on behalf of shorebirds and thousands of ducks and sandhill cranes, which use the playa and its marshy edge as wintering grounds. Thousands of sandhill cranes may arrive in a single flight from as far away as Siberia.

Many Indians of desertlands believe that frogs are created by rain, and in a sense they are right. Rains make little ephemeral puddles under which frog's eggs have been waiting. In the puddles, the eggs hatch and the frogs go through their entire life cycle in a matter of days, depositing more eggs to wait out the next drought. In the playa, much the same process occurs with little marine shrimp that race through sped-up lives in the puddles of summer.

Not far west on I-10, one enters an area that looks eerily as if some giant kid had spilled his marbles on the ground and gone home. Huge quartz monzonite monoliths litter the land, making one wonder how

Above: *A male Merriam's turkey performs a most irresistible display. His ancestors, domesticated by ancient Mexicans, gave rise to all of today's Thanksgiving gobblers as well as to the turkeys of Europe.*

they got there. They are in fact part of the intrusions that formed the **Little Dragoon Mountains** north of the highway, and the **Dragoons❖** to the south. The rocks became jointed and cracked into rectangular blocks, then weathering processes widened the cracks and rounded off the corners. The rock consists of thin layers, and the boulders become rounder as layers peel off (a process called sheeting).

From Route 666 South, a road leads westward into the Dragoons. Just to the south of the range's highest peak, Mount Glenn (7,512 feet), and through a narrow and easily defended canyon, lies **Cochise Stronghold,** where the great Apache leader usually made his summer camp and the forest service maintains a campground today.

Twenty-one miles south of Benson between Routes 80 and 90, Route 82 leads to Fairbank and the headquarters of the **San Pedro Riparian National Conservation Area❖.** These 56,431 acres along the San Pedro River were designed to preserve the most extensive, pristine riparian ecosystem remaining in the desert southwest. The area protects the north-flowing San Pedro from the Mexican border 40 miles north, nearly to the town of St. David. A holding of the Bureau of Land Management, the area offers hiking, camping, and horseback riding beside a peaceful perennial stream that is the only undammed river in Arizona. Along the banks are long reaches of Fremont cottonwood and

Goodding willow, along with Arizona ash and walnut, netleaf hackberry, and soapberry. The uplands on both sides of the river are desert scrubland—tarbush, creosote, and acacia, with mesquite and grass in the bottomlands along the banks. All this variety creates excellent habitat for wildlife, and wildlife abounds—more than 80 mammal species including bobcats, mountain lions, deer, javelina, and many nocturnal rodents. In all more than 350 birds have been spied along the river, more than half of all North American species—including 100 breeders and the rare gray hawk, the crested caracara, the extremely rare green kingfisher, and the northern beardless tyrannulet. Those of a mind to can also seek out the Mojave green rattlesnake.

Above: *The rare lemon lily (Lilium parryi) of Ramsey Canyon was named for nineteenth-century explorer-botanist Charles Parry.*

Right: *In this typically north-south basin-and-range region, Ramsey Creek tumbles eastward out of the Huachuca Mountains, a rare orientation that renders Ramsey Canyon one of the Southwest's lushest riparian zones. The canyon is home to 170 bird species and 300 plant species from tiny mosses to stately Douglas fir.*

Of the various points of entry to the riparian area, one is where Route 90 crosses the river between Sierra Vista and Bisbee. There, a modest visitor center presides over a path through fields to the river and the shade. Wandering along the banks and

onto the pebbly shoals, one can hardly avoid being tailed by a pair of curious vermilion flycatchers.

West of Benson and about a quarter-mile off Route 90 in the Whetstone Mountains lies one of the best-kept secrets in Arizona in many a year, and the newest addition to the Arizona State Parks system, **Kartchner Caverns State Park❖.** In 1974, looking for caves in the Whetstones, a couple of amateur spelunkers poked their heads down a sinkhole from which they could feel a breeze emanating. They got only as far as a 300-foot room filled with stalactites and stalagmites unlike anything they had ever seen. Eventually, explorers discovered there a 13,000-foot world-class cavern containing thousands of stalactites and stalagmites, as well as countless other formations—shields, soda straws, helictites, and bacon. More spectacular, it was a living cave, geopoetry still being written. Eventually the landowner, the Kartchner family, sold the property to the Nature Conservancy, which in turn worked with the state to achieve state park status for it. The arrangements were managed with the utmost secrecy: The existence of the caverns was known to only a handful of people until a couple of years ago. Recently opened to the public after intensive study of its fragile ecosystem, it includes a visitor center, campground, and various nature trails.

ABOVE: *The broad-billed hummingbird is one of several species of hummers—including the magnificent, bluethroated, and violet-crowned—whose only U.S. appearances are in southern Arizona.*

LEFT: *A Gila woodpecker feeds on aloe vera. Conspicuous and noisy, these birds make nests in saguaro holes, which are then used by other bird species.*

All year round, people flock to the Nature Conservancy's **Ramsey Canyon Preserve❖,** at the end of Ramsey

Canyon Road, ten miles south of Sierra Vista on the eastern flank of the Huachuca Mountains. The preserve plays host to a number of truly rare species, such as the recently discovered Ramsey Canyon leopard frog, the Tepic flame flower, and the lemon lily (*Lilium parryi*). But many visitors come for the hummingbirds that appear in this steep, lush canyon, including the rare blue-throated hummingbird. Many are disappointed to find that only in early May and again in August do hummingbird migrations bring peak numbers to Ramsey Canyon, but it is a wondrous place at any time of year.

Access to this popular preserve is limited to protect its fragile habitats, and those who wish to visit in peak season are advised to make reservations well in advance. Reservations are essential to stay in one of the few cabins at the foot of the preserve and be lulled to sleep by the sweetest sound in the entire Southwest, that of water rushing over rocks. The permanent, spring-fed stream that tumbles down this nearly magical canyon provides for sycamores, maples, and columbines along the stream banks, and only a few feet beyond are yuccas, cacti, and agaves. A National Natural Landmark since 1964, the steep-sided canyon itself, running east-west, seems ever moist and cool, a place that in season dances with butterflies, as well as 170 species of avian jewelry and 300 species of plants, from little mosses to huge Douglas firs. One well-marked nature trail follows the creek, leading past a meadow filled with the native range grass called side oats grama, past canyon grapes, horsetails, Emory oaks, a spiny evergreen bush called buckbrush, yuccas, agaves, Arizona oaks, bigtooth maples, alligator junipers, and Arizona walnuts. Yet another, tougher trail leads up into the wilderness area above, part of the Huachuca Mountain range within the **Coronado National Forest❖.**

Like the Chiricahuas, the **Huachuca Mountains** are another classically diverse sky island that harbors much of the same unusual blend of northern and southern species, including such rarities as the lemon lily, the Tepic flame flower, and the lesser long-nosed bat. One little-visited gem in the Huachucas is the **Canelo Hills Cienega Preserve❖,** located along the forest road that leads from Fort Huachuca to Sonoita (precisely, at milepost 16 on Route 83). Owned and managed by the Nature Conservancy, these 205 acres along the permanent O'Donnell Creek contain one of the last few *cienegas* (marshlands) in southern Arizona. Also on site is an 1880s adobe homestead; an outbuilding serves as a visitor sign-in point and contains a modest library. Unique to this cienega is a rare orchid, *Spiranthea graminea,* until recently thought not to occur in the United States. Cottonwoods, willows, and walnuts grow densely along the banks of the creek, and the surround is rolling grassland and oak and juniper woodland—another place where one would hardly be surprised to see a few mastodons come over the horizon. The stream is home for several endangered fish, including the Gila chub and Gila sucker, and the reserve provides critical habitat for the likes of canyon tree frogs, red-spotted toads, and black-tailed rattlesnakes.

A creek runs along Route 82 from Sonoita to Patagonia and beyond; critic and essayist Joseph Wood Krutch once said of this perennial stream, "No other area in Arizona is more deserving of preservation." Running between the Santa Rita and Patagonia mountains through a magnificent grassy valley, the creek is lined with majestic stands of 100-foot Fremont cottonwoods interspersed among Arizona walnuts and velvet ashes, willows, and Texas mulberries. It is generally considered the best remaining example of this kind of riparian habitat, once far more common. And just off the road in Patagonia, a 1.5-mile stretch of the creek and the surrounding 312 acres have been preserved by the Nature Conservancy in the form of the **Patagonia–Sonoita Creek Preserve❖.** A new visitor center greets increasing numbers of travelers partway into the sanctuary along a well-marked trail. Some 200 birds have been noted here, along with a host of other wildlife that includes coatimundis, badgers, Colorado River toads, desert tortoises, and the Southwest's most endangered fish, the Gila topminnow. One may come across a small herd of javelinas feeding at midday on watercress in the spring, or hear the poignant whistle of a gray hawk, one of many mostly Mexican species found here. A National Natural Landmark, it hosts the rose-throated becard and beardless flycatcher, along with its vermilion cousin, Montezuma quail, and in the fall the trees are alive with migrating warblers.

The area considered the ultimate bird-watcher's mecca is north of here in the **Santa Ritas,** in the shadow of Mount Hopkins, where the

OVERLEAF: *Graceful yellow columbine nod over slow-moving water in an intimate natural garden along Sycamore Creek in the Pajarita Wilderness, part of the far-flung Coronado National Forest.*

Smithsonian Institution maintains an astrophysical observatory that includes a huge multimirrored array for probing the universe of infrared. But no astronomer can claim to have scoured the heavens any more sharply than the stream of birders who journey from around the world to **Madera Canyon❖.** This mountain canyon surrounded by desert, a pocket of dense vegetation only about 40 miles south of Tucson, is a mecca also for 200 bird species, many of them extremely rare. For example, recently spotted was a flame-backed tanager, so rare as not to be mentioned at all in the 1978 edition of the standard book *The Birds of Arizona.*

Just north of Sonoita, off Route 83, lie 45,000 acres of ranchland that narrowly avoided becoming a huge development and have been administered since 1988 by the Bureau of Land Management. This is the **Empire Cienega Resource Conservation Area❖,** high rolling grasslands located between the Whetstone and Santa Rita mountains. The lush grass reaches six feet in height in some locations, with a variety of trees breaking up expansive pastures. Cottonwoods, willows, and velvet ashes hug the banks of the permanent Cienega Creek, which rises from a spring and runs about ten miles before returning underground. Along its course it hosts three native fish—the endangered Gila topminnow, the Gila chub, and the longfin dace. The largest Emory oak in the country—43 feet tall, with a 68-foot crown spread—stands like a sentinel in a secluded and unnamed canyon. Wildlife—game and nongame—thrives in this large area of mostly uniform habitat, no paved roads, and mild climate. Hiking, camping, riding, and picnicking are all permitted, but no facilities of any sort are provided because the bureau wishes to maintain the area in its pristine condition.

The Coronado National Forest's 7,420-acre **Pajarita Wilderness** is some 17 miles west of Nogales off Interstate 19 on scenic Route 289. It provides the access to Sycamore Canyon, which some consider one of the most interesting crannies in the state. Not to be confused with the much larger Sycamore canyons near Flagstaff and Payson, this is a steep-sided four-mile canyon in which some 660 different plant species have been identified. A popular place for day hikes, though seldom crowded, it begins at Hank and Yank Spring, named for two early homesteaders. The trail immediately passes some spectacular spires and enters a tree-lined creekbed (which runs infrequently but always leaves standing pools) and the **Goodding Natural Research Area,** named for a botanist who noted the astonishing botanical diversity of the canyon. Farther along, pools, side canyons, and desert plants on the hillsides provide a near wonderland to be explored. One unusual feature of the canyon is that riparian and desert plants and others with widely divergent ecological requirements grow very close together. In all, 17 species occur only here in the United States. One of them, a rare fern known as *Asplenium exiguum,* exists only in Sycamore Canyon, parts of Mexico, and the Himalayas.

TUCSON ENVIRONS

The bustling and still burgeoning city of Tucson takes up most of the valley that lies between the Tucson Mountains on the west and on the east, the Rincon and Santa Catalina mountains. The tallest of these, Mount Lemmon at 9,157 feet, towers above the city. However prominent the mountains are, what strikes most people's eyes as they arrive is the grand "forests" of saguaro cacti, which the **Saguaro National Monument❖** was established to preserve. The monument is in two sections, one some 21,000 acres west in the Tucson Mountains, reached via Kinney Road off Speedway, the other about 66,000 acres to the east, reached via Broadway and Old Spanish Trail. Both districts have excellent visitor centers, roads, and trails, but there are no campgrounds. The eastern block is more diverse, much of it a roadless wilderness rising above 8,000 feet into the mountains.

These huge fluted cacti, which some

ABOVE: *A giant saguaro cactus, which can grow higher than 50 feet, provides convenient nesting space for an evidently indignant elf owl.*

OVERLEAF: *An astonishing diversity characterizes the Sonoran Desert, although its major distinguishing features are the grand saguaro cacti, sentinels that dominate Tucson Mountain Park.*

157

locals call "cucumber trees," can live up to 200 years. They grow from a seed the size of a period on this page to a height of 50 feet or more, weighing in at eight tons. The saguaros bespeak the Sonoran Desert, which some call the "green desert" because it is the youngest and most diverse in plant life. Another oddball plant is the bushy, green-barked palo verde; along with mesquite, it serves as a "nurse plant" under whose protection a saguaro seedling gets its start. Like that wild-looking floozy the ocotillo, the palo verde sprouts its tiny leaves only days after a rainstorm. It drops them as drought sets in again, letting its green bark do the photosynthesizing. Cacti abound: barrel, hedgehog, fishhook, teddybear cholla, prickly pear—testimony to the creativity of this tribe (and those who named them).

But the stately saguaros dominate. By age 50 they may be seven feet tall but reproductively immature. By 75, they begin to sprout some prickly, ball-shaped branches that will grow upward into "arms," and at this time the plant begins to flower. Gila woodpeckers and gilded flickers make holes in these giants, and the plant soon produces a kind of callus that lines the cavities. These holes, called "boots" by the locals, provide dwellings not only for their makers but also for kestrels, Lucy's warblers, cactus wrens, western kingbirds, elf owls, and purple martins (which in the Southwest do not live in colonies as elsewhere). The holes are 20 degrees cooler in summer and 20 degrees warmer in winter than their surroundings. Birds such as Harris' hawks nest on the cacti themselves.

Perfectly adapted to the wayward conditions of the desert, a saguaro's roots generally extend out from the trunk about the same distance as the plant's height. They sprout special root hairs when the ground becomes moist, soaking up as much as 200 gallons of water, a year's supply. Their favored habitat is the bajadas that slope up to mountains.

In summer the saguaro puts forth a juicy figlike fruit that feeds javelinas, coyotes, foxes, rodents, even harvester ants. The fruit has long been a source of jam, syrup, and wine for the Papago Indians, now called by their own name, Tonoho O'odham (Desert People).

Recently there has been concern that in some areas, many saguaros

LEFT: *The blooms of a saguaro cactus presage the appearance of its fruit, which local Indians, the Tonoho O'odham (formerly called the Papago), made into a heady beverage for a sacred annual revelry.*

were dying prematurely and few new ones were growing. Cattle—trampling nurse plants and packing the ground so hard that seeds cannot grow—are no longer a problem in the monument. The many apartment holes for birds do little if anything to harm the cacti. It was determined that the main threat to these plants, which here and to the north reach their northernmost and easternmost limit, is the occasional freezing winter.

There are many ways to experience this monument: by car, on foot, on horseback. One of the better ways is to fetch a picnic dinner from one of Tucson's superb Mexican restaurants and hightail it into the monument's western section. There, one can watch the saguaros, backlit by a reddening sun streaming across an expanse of basin and range that appears never to have felt the step of a human foot, and listen to the coyotes sing their vespers.

Camping in the monument is restricted to six areas in the eastern block. Adjacent to the western block and reached by Gates Pass Road is **Tucson Mountain Park❖,** 18,000 acres of Sonoran Desert well restored to its natural state after cattle grazing was eliminated in 1929. Here one can find plenty of hiking trails, about 150 different campsites for spending a night in the desert, and, surprisingly, solitude.

The best way to prepare oneself for a trip into the Sonoran Desert is to visit the **Arizona–Sonora Desert Museum❖,** located along Kinney Road just outside the monument's western district. More than a museum, it is also a zoo and botanical garden. Here one can see most of the animals and plants that will be encountered (and those that one rarely sees—margays, ocelots, jaguarundis) and learn their life histories and complex interactions, which are at the heart of the green desert. Recently an underground "limestone cave" and a "dry cave" have been added, along with a stunning exhibit of the minerals of the Sonoran Desert. There is a planted textbook reminder of the life zones one encounters moving up in altitude, and two outdoor aviaries where one can sit and associate the birdcalls and songs of the desert with the actual singers. So popular is the museum with the "snowbirds" flocking to Tucson from September to April that it is best to get there early.

RIGHT: *An orphaned and captive-reared mountain lion, freed in the desert near Kitt Peak and obviously undeterred by a photographer's presence, explores an unfamiliar desert "tree," a saguaro cactus.*

Within shooting distance of Tucson is **Sabino Canyon,** a popular tourist spot within the **Coronado National Forest❖.** A shuttle bus plies this scenic canyon, which slices into the forerange of the Catalinas under towering cliffs of lichen-covered gray gneiss banded with white quartz and along a boulder-strewn stream crossed by nine bridges. Stops along the way provide for picnics or day hikes into the **Pusch Ridge Wilderness,** which borders the northern edge of the city.

The hour-long drive up the Catalina Highway (which branches off from East Tanque Verde Road) takes one rapidly through the life zones studied at the Desert Museum. The road curves and dips on its way up to the top of **Mount Lemmon.** This vast granite dome rises above the other local mountains, and from its heavily forested top one can see tier after tier of ragged blue mountain ranges stretching off for a hundred miles. Along the way, beyond mile 14, the road passes the fanciful work of weathering on granite—water, ice, and the roots of plants break down the crystalline structure of the rock, turning it into bizarre pillars and hoodoos, favorite haunts for technical climbers.

It is about a 70-mile trip from Tucson to the **Aravaipa Canyon Wilderness**

LEFT: *Untold volts link a dry earth to heaven's ethereal glow over the Organ Pipe Cactus National Monument. Unpredictable summer storms can unleash sudden violence on the unwary traveler.*

165

Area❖, reached by driving north out of the city on Route 89 to Oracle Junction and taking Route 77 some 8 miles past Mammoth to a well-marked turnoff. Some 19,410 acres in all, it is widely proclaimed a "gem" of the Southwest. The steep-sided, 11-mile canyon, in some places 1,000 feet deep and often so narrow a hiker simply has to wade, hosts the perennial Aravaipa Creek. Here is what many consider the richest riparian habitat in the state, along with desert flora above the riparian zone. Nine side canyons with names like Hell Hole, Booger, and Hells Half Acre lead up to the rim, which is covered with chaparral. The wilderness is especially beautiful in autumn, when the riparian woodlands turn scarlet and gold, blazing against the multicolored canyon walls and the desert plants beyond. Wildlife is teemingly abundant, with 200 species of birds and numerous mammals, including a herd of bighorn sheep that occasionally make a dramatic appearance on the north rim. Entrance is by permit only, and since only 50 people are allowed in the area at any one time, reservations should be made up to three months in advance. There are no trails, and campgrounds are primitive at best: This is, after all, a wilderness. The canyon can be hiked in a day, but most people stay for at least one of the two nights permitted.

Approximately 50 miles southwest of Tucson, off Route 286, is **Buenos Aires National Wildlife Refuge❖.** These 114,500 acres of grassland in the Altar Valley were once counted among the largest cattle ranches in the state. The refuge was set aside specifically to save the endangered masked bobwhite quail, abundant before overgrazing and drought near the turn of the century eliminated most of its habitat in the southern part of the state. Although the quail are elusive, a hiker or driver along the 10-mile self-guided road may well see mule and Coues white-tailed deer, pronghorns, javelinas, and a variety of water and marsh birds. One can roam and camp but there are no facilities.

On the horizon to the west is the Bureau of Land Management's **Baboquivari Peak Wilderness❖.** The area encompasses a portion of the narrow and sinuous Baboquivari Range, which rises sharply from

---

RIGHT: *In one of the world's more arid places, Organ Pipe Cactus National Monument, spring-flowering brittlebush proves that the desert needs no artificial irrigation to bloom abundantly.*

ABOVE: *A quartet of curious bighorn sheep observe the observer, unaware that they live in what has been called a sparkling gem of the southwestern desert, the Aravaipa Canyon Wilderness Area.*

the surrounding desert, dominated by the massive granite, turretlike dome of Baboquivari Peak (7,730 feet). Visible from miles and miles around, the peak is sacred to the Tohono O'odham (Papago Indians), whose vast, arid reservation lies west of the mountains. It is a rugged hike up to the crest, with spectacular vistas as a reward. But to scale the dome itself is a Grade 6, Class 6 technical haul and the only one in the state that takes more than a day.

THE ARID ZONE

Heading west, one crosses the Tohono O'odham Reservation (their other appellation, Papago, was given them by the Spanish and means "bean eater"). The Tohono O'odham are noted for their exquisite basketry, and it is worth stopping off in any of the scattered villages to

ABOVE: *Long fingers of the aptly named organ-pipe cactus seem to point toward the sky, where the glorious colors of sunset are about to spread above Organ Pipe Cactus National Monument.*

acquire one or more baskets.

The land that stretches from the eastern edge of the reservation, marked by the rugged bastion of the Ajo Mountains, all the way to Yuma on the California border is considered the heart of the Sonoran Desert. And if a heart can itself have a heart, that is **Organ Pipe Cactus National Monument✧,** where, in some 330,000 acres, the Sonoran Desert can be seen in its most extravagant variety. In the eastern portion are all of the desert types found in Saguaro National Monument—the saguaro, fishhook, barrel, and other cacti, palo verde, mesquite, ironwood—but also the bizarre cactus, occurring only in this vicinity, for which the monument was named. This relative of the saguaro looks for all the world like a pipe organ without a keyboard. But instead of a single trunk with branches, it has many thick arms that

169

grow from a cluster at the base, sometimes achieving a height of 20 feet. The surrounding terrain varies from rolling hills to sandy washes in deep arroyos and volcanic peaks jutting on the horizon.

Although 95 percent of the monument is a roadless wilderness area, two graded loop roads leave Route 85 at the visitor center, which is 4 miles north of the Mexican border crossing at Lukeville. One can also enter the monument from the north, taking Route 85 south from the town of Why. Ajo Mountain Drive, 21 miles in length, runs to the east through classic organ-pipe cactus desert. Puerto Blanco Drive, a 53-mile westerly loop, swings down along the border; across the border one can see elephant trees and Senita cactus. This desert type stretches south to the Gulf of California coast. A different desert type occurs in the western end of the monument, where most plants have small leaves, like creosote bush.

There are several trails in addition to the loop roads. One, the Quitobaquito Trail, leads to springs of the same name and a small pond with a marshy edge that is one of the few oases in this vast stretch of arid land. The springs will in season host hundreds of different kinds of water- and shorebirds: In all the monument bird list contains 275 species. Deer and coyotes can be seen, particularly near dusk. The springs are also the only known habitat of the endangered desert pupfish.

One of the most forbidding and intriguing places in the United States lies west of the monument, **Cabeza Prieta National Wildlife Refuge❖,** some 860,000 acres of the Sonoran Desert's hottest, driest, and toughest terrain. The road that crosses through it from just north of Organ Pipe Cactus National Monument on the way to Yuma is called El Camino del Diablo, the Devil's Highway, for the thousands of people, mostly afflicted with gold fever, who perished along its course. In 1896, a surveyor wrote of the road, "It is hard to imagine a more desolate and depressing ride." There was, he said, "little to distract the eye from the awful surrounding dreariness and desolation except the bleaching skeletons of horses and the painfully frequent crosses which mark the graves of those who perished of thirst." The travelers were

---

RIGHT: *Dawn gilds a rain-filled natural catchment in Tinajas Altas, a rare sight at the western end of usually water-starved Cabeza Prieta National Wildlife Refuge. None of the water, however, is drinkable.*

unable to find one of the few rain catchments (called *tinajas*) and even fewer springs. Today, none of the water to be found in the handful of wells and wildlife tanks in the refuge is potable.

If that description is not sufficiently discouraging, one might be put off by the fact that more than half the refuge is within the Luke Air Force Gunnery Range. Even to enter the refuge, visitors must obtain a permit at Ajo and sign a military hold-harmless agreement. Requests for permits must be made three weeks ahead of time, so that the Air Force can check the schedule to see if would-be top guns will be practicing their explosive arts, in which case the refuge is closed altogether. In all, only a couple of hundred permits are requested each year, and not even the few desert rats who leave the Devil's Highway for a bit of hiking go there in the summer.

LEFT: *The Imperial National Wildlife Refuge attracts teeming hosts of passing seabirds including this astonishing, if temporary, barrio of cormorants.*

The refuge was established in 1939 to preserve bighorn sheep, and the region's numerous mountain ranges—such as the Growlers, the Cabezo Prietas (black head), and the Tinajas Altas (high tanks)—are highly suitable for these animals. A few hundred remain but are rarely seen. In addition, the endangered Sonoran pronghorn and a host of other desert creatures make a living here, coexisting with the occasional delivery of ordnance into their midst. Lava flows lick across some of the valleys; creosote and bursage predominate in the basins, but cacti similar to those in the national monument to the east creep up the bajadas. Because it has been so little used for so long, except in the bombing range areas, the desert is in excellent condition.

After about 85 miles, the Devil's Highway leaves the refuge and enters the western half of the Barry M. Goldwater Range, administered by the U.S. Marines, and arrives at **Tinajas Altas❖** (for which the mountains were named), a series of granite cups along a spillway and the most reliable water source anywhere in the region. Some call it the most important desert water hole in the United States, and it is much appreciated by bighorn sheep and other wildlife. The highway, navigable with four-wheel drive, continues to take its toll nevertheless. Along the stretch north of Tinajas Altas, hundreds of Mexicans, having struggled across the border headed for Interstate 8 and a new life, have perished in recent years. For the hardy (and well equipped), the trip through Cabeza Prieta refuge is well worth it, if only to be able to say one has done it.

After such a journey, the soul pleads for the sight of water. It can be

ABOVE: *Unexpected interlopers in the Sonoran landscape of Kofa National Wildlife Refuge, the native palm trees of Arizona draw many to marvel at one of their two unforgiving and fragile homes.*

found in Yuma, which sits on a rise above the Colorado River, where, historically, it was safe from the river's periodic floods. Today, the river's water is so heavily used upstream, so tamed and channelized, that floods no longer occur. Instead, what water makes its way locally back into the river from aquifers is so tainted with salts that it must be desalinated at a Bureau of Reclamation plant east of Yuma before flowing into the agricultural lands of Mexico between Yuma and the Gulf of Mexico. Northeast of Yuma and northwest of the Gila Mountains, **Mittry Lake Wildlife Area❖** lies in the flood plain of the Colorado River. This three-mile-long lake, managed by the Arizona Game and Fish Department, was created on behalf of fish and wildlife whose habitat was marred by the channelization of the Colorado. Frequented mostly by anglers, the lush area hosts thousands of water-fowl, shorebirds, and marsh birds and, in the more than 3,000 acres surrounding the lake, numerous songbirds.

From the Imperial Dam, about 20 miles north of Yuma, up beyond the little town of Cibola, the Colorado flows through two contiguous refuges, the **Cibola National Wildlife Refuge❖** in the north and the **Imperial National Wildlife Refuge❖** in the south. Together they comprise some 38,000 acres, mostly in Arizona and mostly river bottomlands and desert created to provide habitat for wintering Canada geese when the river was channelized. But more than 230 bird species are to be seen in these two refuges, including the endangered Yuma clapper rail (if one is sharp-eyed) and even Forster's and black terns, along with a host of shorebirds, marsh birds, and songbirds. The area is alive with rabbits, mice, muskrats, foxes, raccoons, mule deer, bighorn sheep, and a sizable list of whiptail lizards and snakes. Most of the refuge's users come to boat and fish, particularly in the summer; the best months for admiring the wildlife are from November to March. In Imperial NWR this is best done by canoe, either in the new channel or in the original channel.

Due east of these refuges and directly east of Route 95 is the huge 660,000-acre **Kofa National Wildlife Refuge❖,** a largely unspoiled area consisting chiefly of the King Valley, flanked on the north by the large mountain mass of the Kofa Mountains and on the south by the equally rugged but more defined Castle Dome range. Aside from a few signs of Native American use, people shunned the Kofa Mountains until the 1890s, when prospectors began hunting for gold. Supplies and other freight shipments arrived at the King of Arizona mine in crates often bearing the abbreviation KofA—thus the name.

The refuge was set aside for a small herd of bighorn sheep that has since swelled to some 800. Creatures of tradition, the desert bighorns have etched trails into the high ground and these, for those who spot them, make good if rugged hiking paths up into the mountains. The top of Signal Peak, the highest of the range at 4,877 feet, can be reached by a strenuous climb. For those up to that activity it provides a stunning vista of Arizona's western desert and, across the tiny ribbon of the Colorado, California's Mojave Desert. Lesser views occur lower down, where the Palm Canyon Trail peters out. In any case, solo trips are discouraged.

Palm Canyon is the chief draw to the refuge: People drive from hundreds of miles around to take a brief one-mile hike from the end of Palm Canyon Road, 18 miles south of Quartzsite off Route 95. This is

RIGHT: *Engineers tamed the lower Colorado River, providing temporary habitat for great blue herons (such as the one shown here), 230 other bird species, and various fauna and flora as well as farmland. In the Southwest, the proper use of water is the central question facing the human intellect.*

one of only two natural habitats in Arizona for the native palm, *Washingtonia filifera.* Some 40 trees grow in the steep drainages above Palm Canyon, an extraordinary presence in this otherwise fairly typical Sonoran landscape. The other site, at Castle Hot Springs, is on private land.

The rest of the refuge is rugged and rough, four-wheel drive country, best explored with a map. It attracts people with interests quite different from those of hikers and campers: rock hounds. Some nine miles south of Palm Canyon Road, another road enters the refuge at Stone Cabin. About six miles in, it curves south for seven miles, where another road leads west into the **Castle Dome Range.** Here people have found fire agates, which may be picked up from the ground, but not dug for.

To the north, the small town of Quartzsite periodically draws thousands and thousands of people in RVs who come to buy, sell, and trade minerals, staying in a few campsites around town in the desert. The desert here, called **La Posa Plain** and administered by the Bureau of Land Management, is the driest part of Arizona with a trivial three to five inches of rain annually. North, where Route 95 meets Route 72, lies an enormous stretch of sand dunes—in all, some 84,000 acres—called **Cactus Plain❖.** For the most part, the dunes are stabilized by various dune plants, such as Mormon tea and sand spurge. One can wander at will in the rolling terrain of this Bureau of Land Management holding, but a compass is recommended.

When Parker Dam was built just north of Parker and created Lake Havasu, the **Havasu National Wildlife Refuge❖** was established to compensate for the loss of wildlife habitat. Of its two separate units,

the most northerly is **Topock Marsh,** north of Interstate 40, where hundreds of bird species are to be seen. Canada geese arrive in early November, and in the spring there are great rookeries of cormorants and great blue herons. The bulrushes and cattails of the marsh are also important for the endangered and highly secretive subspecies, the Yuma clapper rail. Below the Topock Bridge, the **Topock Gorge Unit** includes what many consider the most scenic part of the lower Colorado, an excellent 16-mile trip by canoe into Lake Havasu. One of the most delightful canoeing tours in the West, it includes a 7-mile

stretch through the multicolored cliffs of Mojave Canyon.

The **Bill Williams River National Wildlife Refuge❖**, almost 4,500 acres, is located on the delta of the Bill Williams River as it eases into the Colorado. Here is one of the last remaining stands of Fremont cottonwoods in the region, along with marshland, saguaros and their cousins, mesas with creosote bush, and high, barren rock desert. Most of the river, east 16 miles to **Alamo Lake State Park❖**, is public land and can be hiked, taking one through steep canyons and across flood plains that lie between the Rawhide and Buckskin mountains.

Alamo Lake, created to control floods, is intensively used by boaters and campers. Beyond the surrounding hills are largely wild mountains. Upstream, above the confluence of the Big Sandy and Santa Maria rivers, is a vast area of Bureau of Land Management land called **Arrastra Mountain Wilderness Area❖**. Here, in addition to Sonoron Desert scrub, one sees Joshua trees and bladder sage, components of the Mojave Desert. Cottonwood bosques occur along the rivers. The floral diversity is matched by a great variety of wildlife, especially birds.

North of Lake Havasu City and the Fort Mojave Indian Reservation is the southern end of the gargantuan **Lake Mead National Recreation Area❖**, chiefly two heavily used large lakes (Mojave and Mead) created by two dams (Davis and Hoover). The Mojave, Sonoran, and Great Basin deserts meet here, and there are a surprising variety of plants and animals, including a large population of desert bighorn sheep. Most people using the recreation area enter it from Nevada.

East from Davis Dam, via Route 68 through Kingman and then about 12 miles southeast on Hualapai Mountain Road, a gem of a county park awaits. **Hualapai Mountain Park❖** is a dramatic leave-taking from the heat of the desert. The park offers cabins, picnic and camping areas, a few trails, and a lot of rugged mountain wilderness. At the park's boundary, one is already some 1,500 feet above the desert floor. A steep, curving road leads one quickly up into mountain forestlands. Hualapai Peak, at 8,417 feet, towers almost a mile above the desert below. One is now in another part of Arizona altogether: the Highlands.

LEFT: *The message of the vista from Grapevine Mesa near the Arizona border overlooking Lake Mead in the distance: Air (the sky), earth (the rock), fire (the sun), and water are all it takes for the miracle of life.*

CHAPTER SIX

THE HIGHLANDS: CENTRAL-WESTERN ARIZONA

T he Central Highlands extend diagonally like a great thumb pointing northwest almost all the way across the state. They comprise a great jumble of mostly rugged mountains and relatively small basins that separate the desert country of the south and west from the high flat plateau in the north. The area is sometimes called the Transition zone, a role best observed on its southwestern edge, where the familiar alluvial fans and desert vegetation climbing the sloping *bajadas* are to be seen, but it has its own unique character. The wettest part of the state, its mountains are cut by innumerable streams and host many lakes, all but one man-made. The more ample rainfall allows much of the Highlands to be heavily forested with pinyon and juniper and, higher up, large stands of ponderosa pines and Douglas firs.

The region has seen mountains come and go, including some really ancient ones great enough to rival today's Himalayas. As always, they have eroded away only to rise again through the incomprehensibly gigantic forces of plate tectonics and vulcanism. The current mountains arose 7 to 13 million years ago and are still being worn away. Not until Pleistocene times were the valleys filled enough

LEFT: *Site of countless old western movie river crossings, Oak Creek Canyon slides like a hymn of praise north of Cathedral Rock, a landmark near the town of Sedona in the heart of red rock country.*

(some with 3,000 feet of fill) to enable local streams to cut through into other valleys, creating a network of drainages that flow into the Gila River and thence to the Colorado. Fossils of the time suggest an area of high lakes and lush savanna among the peaks, roamed by herds of camels and antelopes, mastodons, and others.

The Highlands are dotted with towns large and small, live and ghostly—testimony mostly to a century of mining in places like Prescott, Jerome, and Globe, which began in the 1860s. The first stampede of treasure-seekers found some fairly rich lodes of gold and silver, but the chief ore that ultimately sustained the region was copper. Most of the mines are now closed. Today there is very little privately owned land in the Highlands; the vast proportion is held as national forest, national wilderness, national monument, or Indian reservation.

NORTH OF PHOENIX

There is no way to reach, or leave, Prescott, once the territorial capital, without driving on a scenic road, especially if one patrols the backcountry roads through the Bradshaw Mountains, the western part of **Prescott National Forest❖**. Of all of them, perhaps the most spectacular is the Senator Highway between Prescott and Horsethief Basin. The Bradshaws were long considered impenetrable (until the lure of gold overcame the notion), and they are the most rugged range in central Arizona. The road, built in increments over its early years as miners pressed farther into the mountains from Prescott, runs some 40 miles through steep twisting canyons, mountain peaks, and ravines. At about mile 6 (out of Prescott) and just beyond the Groom Creek store is an old school and a nature trail for the disabled. From about mile 11 to the junction with Walker Road, the narrow, rough road is carved out of the side of a mountain. A one-mile detour up Walker Road brings one to what many consider the most beautiful mountain lake in the state, **Hassayampa Lake,** a jewel nestled in the forest. Also at the junction, a 2.5-mile road leads up **Mount Union,** the highest of the Bradshaws at just under 8,000 feet, from which the panorama is unparalleled. To the northeast, San Francisco Peaks rise to 12,000 feet in the sky; to the east, the silver stream of the Verde River slides by; southeast lie the Mazatzal Mountains. To the west are the Weaver Mountains, and 100 miles beyond those is the Colorado River.

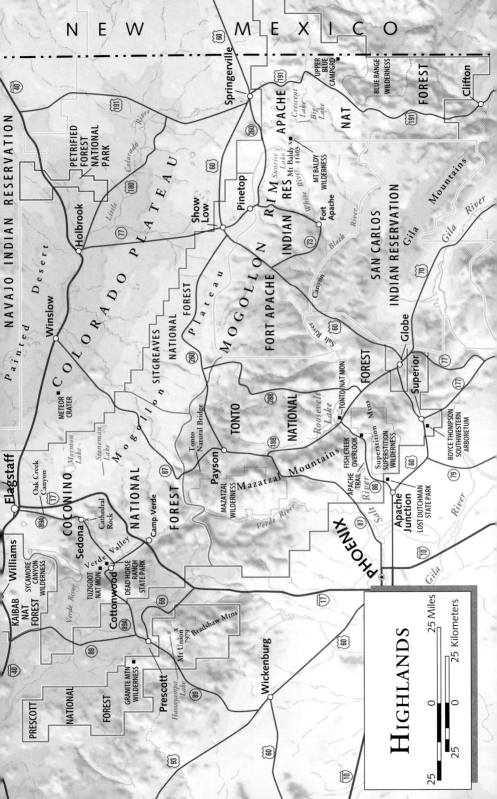

The Senator Highway winds through some chaparral country, rises back up into ponderosa forests to Crown King, and switchbacks down to Cleator, one of the most winding roads anywhere and also the approximate path of an old railroad that came to be known locally as Frank Murphy's Impossible Bradshaw Mountain Railroad.

The Prescott National Forest contains eight wilderness areas, one of which, **Castle Creek Wilderness,** lies near Crown King; a climb up to Juniper Ridge provides a magnificent view of the central Arizona desert. Another, **Granite Mountain Wilderness,** is about eight miles northwest of Prescott. Some 10,000 acres, it is mostly a single, isolated mountain strewn with boulders and slabs, rising 2,000 feet above its surround to an elevation of 7,626 feet; its 500-foot-high granite southwest face is popular with technical climbers. For non climbers, a fairly straightforward trail leaves from Granite Mountain Road and leads to Blaine Pass; from there it is one mile to the summit and another panoramic vista.

Northeast, on Alternate 89, lies the town of Cottonwood, and just across the Verde River is **Dead Horse Ranch State Park❖,** a campground and an excellent headquarters for exploring this beautiful riparian area, lined with cottonwoods and other vegetation that attracts a wide variety of birds. Most of the Verde is protected as a wild and scenic river, and beginning at Camp Verde, it is a popular rafting stream. Not far downstream from the state park lies **Tuzigoot National Monument❖,** chiefly an archaeological site devoted to a pueblo-style village that once flourished here and has been partly restored. Its original inhabitants, today called the Sinagua, lived from here up to the San Francisco Mountains; the Hopi Indians believe that the Sinagua comprised some of their early clans. According to their history, prophecy caused early Hopi groups from all around the region to migrate to their present home, three arid mesas 90 miles east of Flagstaff. A Hopi priest, visiting the Tuzigoot ruin perched above the river, said: "This was a real nice place. It's too bad we had to leave it." The monument has published a checklist of birds that can be seen here and, after visiting the ruin, it is a real nice, and quiet, place to wander with a pair of binoculars.

LEFT: *A windblown ponderosa and a thunderhead perform a graceful pas de deux at a rocky headland of Mount Union in the Prescott National Forest's Bradshaw Mountains, in Arizona's highlands.*

The **Verde Valley** is another one of Arizona's geological wonders. It has been called a kind of geological no-man's-land between the highlands of the Black Mountain range and the Mogollon Rim, at the edge of the Colorado Plateau, because it is neither one nor the other. Farther north on Route 89A, beyond an area of rich desert grasslands, is the fast-growing town of **Sedona,** one of the state's most popular resort areas and for good reason. In this quintessential red rock country, some ancient event deposited an especially thick layer of bright red and (in places) erosion-resistant rock. The rock, probably a wind-laid sandstone, has since been carved by wind and water into a phantasmagoria of awesome shapes—temples, mesas in the slow process of becoming buttes, buttes becoming pinnacles, and pinnacles on the way to oblivion. There are several arches, countless hoodoos, and old Indian ruins here and there in high caves. Pygmy forests of pinyon, oneseed and Utah juniper, and Arizona cypress reach up the sides of the mesas, a green blanket clinging to the vertiginous red rock that, glowing in the late afternoon sun, leaves one breathless.

Several species of yucca occur here, and scattered across the rocky slopes are green rosettes of long succulent spiky leaves, often called century plants. When these agaves are ready to bloom, they send up a rapidly growing naked stalk on top of which yellow flowers soon and briefly blossom. After this single bout of flowering, the plant dies. In all, there are a whopping 550 different seed plants in the 500 square miles of the Sedona region, along with 180 bird species and 55 mammals. Lower Oak Creek—below town where it slips over flat rock amid cottonwood and sycamore stands, past a great red temple called **Cathedral Rock❖**—is a popular place for birders (and the scene of many old western movies). People of a psychic bent have found eight places in the area, among them Cathedral Rock, that emit tremendous energy; they are known locally as vortices.

The town—filled with galleries, gee-gaw stores, boutiques, restaurants, and fancy resort hotels—is too crowded for some tastes. But virtually any youthful salesperson will explain his or her favorite hiking trails out of town and up into the red rocks. For the less athletic, one of the guided commercial Jeep trips into the hills is highly rewarding. Or one can drive up Schnebley Hill Road, reached from the south by not crossing the bridge in the middle of town but by turning right instead. Paved for a mile, the road winds through Bear Wallow Canyon and twists up the mountain's face (closed in winter). There are various turnouts along the way and huge areas of largely flat red rimrock, excellent for a meditative stroll among the distant mesas looming above. The view from Schnebley Hill Vista, some 1,800 feet above the town, with bizarre and serene red mesas and deep green valleys stretching away for miles, should be accompanied by a philharmonic orchestra.

Down the east side of the mountains, a six-mile stretch of gravel road meets Interstate 17. Two miles north, a turnoff at Mund's Park leads to **Mormon Lake** beyond the aspen-topped, 8,440-foot peak of Mormon Mountain. The lake, within the **Coconino National Forest❖,** is a highly popular recreation place where the Forest Service maintains several campgrounds. A bit south, little **Stoneman Lake,** probably the only "natural" lake in the state, lies in a bowl. There are some summer houses along its shore, but there is also good fishing.

North and east is one of the country's oddest geological formations, what one observer called a "strange freak of nature, a mountain canted on its side." Actually formed by folding and faulting of the earth's crust, this is the most prominent section of the **Mogollon Rim,** which runs all the way from the New Mexico border to the Lake Mead area, the defining boundary between the Highlands and the Colorado Plateau. It is not visible as a rim along its entire course; but in one stretch of 42 miles, north of Payson between Arizona Routes 87 and 260, it rises up, a towering battlement as much as 2,000 feet above the Tonto Basin to the south. The **Rim Road** begins north of Strawberry off Route 87 and passes through a region offering some of the most varied trees and plants in the Coconino National Forest—including a host of summer wildflowers and shady glens filled with tall grass and, unexpectedly, ferns. At various points along the way—such as Kehl Springs campground and in particular, Hi-View Point—are spectacular views from the rim out across the Tonto Basin and the rolling sea of the Highlands. The road dips down into General Springs Canyon, then rises again into country high enough to host a few Engelmann spruces. To the north, various canyons have

OVERLEAF: *Called "Madonna" and the "Praying Nuns," these glowing sandstone pinnacles south of the resort town of Sedona light up as if from within in an end-of-the-day embrace of the glowing sun.*

been dammed to provide fishing, and there are numerous campgrounds along the way. Twelve miles down from the rim on Route 260, a turnoff at Kohl's Ranch leads to the site of Zane Grey's cabin, where he wrote several harum-scarum novels about this part of the world. The structure was destroyed in the tragic "Dude" forest fire of 1990.

TONTO NATIONAL FOREST

Scholars have vainly tried to determine the tribe of the Lone Ranger's faithful Indian companion, Tonto. Fran Striker, creator of the resourceful masked rider of the Plains, never said. One could assume he was a Tonto Apache, a band of western Apache that roamed the Arizona Highlands, but in one novel Tonto could not understand the similar dialect of the Chiricahua Apache. So Tonto couldn't have been a Tonto. The key might lie in Tonto's famous form of address, "Kemo Sabe." One scholar found in the lexicon of the Tewa Indians from New Mexico the words *sabe* and *kema*—meaning Apache and friend. If one allows the word Apache to have slipped to the word *faithful,* Tonto was a Tewa. Another scholar said he was a Yavapai, a western Arizona tribe that often intermingled with the Tonto Apache. If Striker mistakenly asked a Yavapai how to say "man in white clothes," he would have replied "kinmsabeh." So Tonto was a Yavapai. Maybe. At any rate, **Tonto National Forest❖** was certainly named for the Apache.

Almost three million acres in extent, it is near enough to Phoenix to be heavily used, but it contains several wilderness areas: About a fifth of its total area is roadless wilderness. Tonto National Forest ranges from Sonoran Desert scrub to mixed conifer at the highest elevations of its many rugged ranges. One of its attractions is found between the towns of Pine and Payson three miles west of Route 87: **Tonto Natural Bridge,** which towers 183 feet above Pine Creek and is said to be the world's largest travertine arch bridge. Natural flows deposited the travertine and later streams attacked it, forming the arch. The creek flows under the arch and into a deep pool; nearby are several caves with travertine stalactites and stalagmites.

LEFT: *In the Red Rock Secret Mountain Wilderness, Capitol Butte commands the horizon. At its foot, a grove of century plants (agave), manzanita, and a stalwart juniper tree provide touches of green.*

ABOVE: *Call it cougar, puma, panther, or catamount, the mountain lion is rarely seen but seems to hold its own nowadays in the highland Southwest after years of heavy hunting.*

RIGHT: *La Barge Canyon stretches below Battleship Mountain in the Superstition Mountains, a dangerous range east of Phoenix and home of the legendary Lost Dutchman gold mine.*

For serious backpackers with a yen for the largely undisturbed wild, the last stronghold of the much-feared Tonto Apache is the place—the 250,000-acre **Mazatzal Wilderness** west and south of Payson, with most trailheads reached from Route 87. Mazatzal is a Paiute Indian term meaning "empty place in between," and the wilderness is framed by the steep escarpment of the Mazatzal Mountains on the east and the Verde River Valley on the west. Cougars and bears roam this wilderness, and mule deer, javelinas, and coyotes are often seen. The various ecosystems—from Sonoran Desert along the river, through chaparral, pinyon-juniper, and up to Douglas fir—are in especially good condition

in this least-used part of the Tonto Forest. Truly a wilderness, this area is not for the inexperienced. To the east near the mountains are steep, rugged canyonlands; to the west are rolling but very remote areas. Barnhardt Trailhead, reached by Barnhardt Road (which goes west off Route 87 about 14 miles south of Payson), is a popular one. Its trails lead off 7 miles to a high secluded basin and 6 miles to the Mazatzal Divide, which lies beyond rugged cliffs and seasonally a waterfall. Longer treks cross the mountains all the way through the heart of the wilderness to the Verde River.

Just east of Apache Junction are the **Superstition Mountains** with-

193

in the 160,000-acre **Superstition Wilderness.** An ideal base for hikers and horse riders headed for the mountains, the small (320 acres) **Lost Dutchman State Park❖** provides picnic and campgrounds adjoining the National Forest and a new system of trails. Technically a desert range and not part of the Highlands, the Superstitions are at the southern end of the Tonto National Forest. Also called the Killer Mountains, the range is the legendary home of the famed (and almost surely apocryphal) Lost Dutchman Mine, a fabulous vein of gold for which more than 50 seekers are rumored to have killed each other in this century alone. The notion of killers, however, seems to have arisen from the unearthly howls and shrieks of the winds that slam into the southwestern side of the mountains from time to time, screaming in and out of caves and crevices. There is a fair amount of relatively flat Sonoran Desert in the Superstitions, but steep high peaks and deep narrow canyons are the order of the day. So rough are these mountains that the place has remained a wilderness in spite of its proximity to Phoenix. The eastern half is higher in elevation—some 6,000 feet—than the west (2,000 feet in some canyons), but both are uncomfortably hot in the summer months, when sudden thunderstorms can produce flash floods.

People tend to get lost in these rugged mountains, but not those who keep an eye out for the most noticeable landmark, **Weaver's Needle.** Also called the Finger of God and, by the Indians, a scatalogical name having to do with equine prowess, this dark neck of cooled, exposed magma was once the interior of a now-eroded mountain. Protected at its base by crevices, talus slopes, ravines, and cliffs chockablock with a host of spiny desert plants like cacti and catclaw (very aptly named), it pokes up from a jumble of mountains and ridges and bluffs, towering hundreds of feet above its surround. One can walk to the base of Weaver's Needle, but from there on up, alpine equipment is necessary. Regrettably, the 360-degree panorama from the top is often obscured by smog from Phoenix and various nearby smelters.

Located approximately 60 miles east of Phoenix on Route 60 and cradled by the slopes of Picket Post Mountain, the **Boyce Thompson Southwestern Arboretum❖** is a testament to nature's creativity in the face of trying conditions—in this case, fewer than 20 inches of rain annually. It was founded in the 1920s by a mining magnate who wanted to create "the most beautiful and the most useful desert garden of its

Above: *Reaching two feet in length, the Gila monster likes sandy places, where it bites both predator and prey, as well as incautious campers, adding venom to injuries that are rarely fatal—to humans.*

kind in the world." It has become a wonderland of oddities from around the world, but chiefly from the Sonoran Desert. What looks like a normal pine tree of some sort with needles, and pine cones fallen on the ground, is in fact an Australian she-oak, and not a conifer at all. The cones littering the ground are actually fallen flowers. Every sort of cactus imaginable has been planted here, including a variety of chollas, among them "jumping" cholla, so called because newcomers often swear the cacti reached out to spike their legs as they passed by. What seem to be giant upside-down parsnips are in fact boojum trees from the Mexican

Overleaf: *The Superstition Mountains lie in a rugged wilderness area not far from Phoenix. In this century some 50 gold seekers have killed each other there in quest of the fabled Lost Dutchman treasure.*

195

Sonoran Desert. There are two marked trails, one short and one that leads up into rocks and cacti through what almost seem to be natural copses of trees and takes a good two hours' worth of mooning along.

A creek runs through the park, creating a desert riparian area dominated by ashes, walnuts, cottonwoods, desert brooms, and feathery-leaved burrobushes, along with desert willows (which aren't willows, one learns, but relatives of the trumpet vine). Elsewhere "useful" plants are on display—the jojoba bush, whose wax is used in cosmetics and industrial lubricants; the guayule, a bush that is a source of rubber; a variety of yuccas, or Spanish daggers, long used by southwestern Indians for brushes and brooms; and drought-resistant fruit trees, including oranges, pomegranates, and dates. Most of the arboretum's 2,800 plant species bloom until frost (November, typically), but from April through the summer the palette of color is nearly unimaginable and the perfume intoxicating. Many of the same plants can be purchased and taken home for a Xeriscaped garden.

For those camping at Lost Dutchman State Park who seek watery vistas rather than the desert mountain landscape of the Superstitions, an excursion to the **Apache Trail** is the answer. Teddy Roosevelt claimed that this road, which leads from Apache Junction to the man-made lake named for him, was "one of the most spectacular best-worth-seeing sights of the world." About 50 miles long, this section of Route 88 parallels the course of the Salt River, now thoroughly tamed by dams into a chain of reservoirs and lakes, impoundments that made the growth of Phoenix possible in this century. The road passes by the Superstition Mountains and through classic Sonoran Desert country. Two miles west of the state park, **Weaver's Needle Vista** provides an excellent view of this legendary pinnacle. After that the road begins to "twist like a snake with appendicitis" as one writer put it, climbing and descending from ridge to ravine with switchbacks by the dozen. A few miles along, there is a spectacular vista of Canyon Lake, and the road crosses several creeks before reaching the small town of Tortilla Flat (named for a rock formation near Tortilla Creek, and the source of the

---

LEFT: *Weaver's Needle is one of the less scatological names given to this pinnacle in the Superstition Mountains. A technical climber's challenge, the needle is seen here from the Peralta Canyon Trail.*

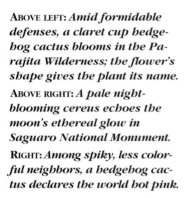

ABOVE LEFT: *Amid formidable defenses, a claret cup hedgehog cactus blooms in the Parajita Wilderness; the flower's shape gives the plant its name.*

ABOVE RIGHT: *A pale night-blooming cereus echoes the moon's ethereal glow in Saguaro National Monument.*

RIGHT: *Among spiky, less colorful neighbors, a hedgehog cactus declares the world hot pink.*

title of John Steinbeck's novel). Five miles later, the pavement ends and a washboardy but maintained dirt road takes over.

About halfway along the Apache Trail's 50 miles is **Fish Creek Overlook** and one of the most astounding descents anywhere. In the old days, when stagecoaches arrived at this point, the driver would fire three shots in the air. A teamster would then arrive and rig a mule team to the *back* of the stage; the mules, facing Phoenix, would act as a backward-walking brake. The descent twists and turns, often hugging the side of the hill, for one and a half hair-raising miles, and crosses a one-lane bridge at the bottom. Beyond, the road winds past Apache Lake for ten miles and then suddenly arrives on a shelf cut from the cliff, where there is a view of Roosevelt Dam, the largest masonry arch dam in the world, built of native stone. Lake Roosevelt, like the other reservoirs on the Apache Trail, is popular with campers, boaters, and fishermen, most of whom avoid the Fish Creek descent and drive here the long way via Globe. At present the height of the dam is being increased, causing a major enlargement of the lake itself.

200

The Apache Trail continues to the turnoff to **Tonto National Monument❖,** located in the southern end of the Mazatzal Mountains, which lie north of the trail for most of its length. From the visitor center there is a fine view of Lake Roosevelt and a trail, with well-labeled plants along the way, leading through some rough talus to the ruins—inhabited by Salado Indians some 900 years ago. However improbably, this area was once a seabed: Fossils called stromatolites (mounds formed from growing algae) have been found in some of the older rocks here. At about a billion years of age, they are among the oldest fossils known.

EASTERN HIGHLANDS

Most of the highlands and desert mountains of central Arizona were until little more than a century ago the largely exclusive realm of the Apache. The drive north of Globe on Route 77 (which simply turns into Route 60 along the way) leads into current Apache country. It is properly shown on most road maps as a scenic drive (although except for a few highways near the major cities, every road in Arizona and New Mexico is scenic), and except for a few still-operating mining towns that make one appreciate the scenery even more, the label is appropriate. Nowhere is it more spectacular than when it switchbacks out of the San Carlos Apache Reservation 2,000 feet down into **Salt River Canyon❖,** a 32,800-acre wilderness and an astounding gorge that can well be considered a mini–Grand Canyon. A bridge takes one across the river to a steep ascent into White Mountain Tribal Lands.

The headwaters of the Salt River arise in the White Mountains to the east, becoming truly the Salt River at the magnificent confluence of the White and Black rivers. From its point of origin near Mount Baldy, the river descends some 10,000 feet on its 200-mile course to Phoenix. Expert kayakers, having obtained permission from the Fort Apache Indian Reservation, sometimes put in a few miles up Black River. The first 15 miles are class II–III in difficulty, but after that things begin to get wild, with 15-foot drops as the river cuts into the rock of Salt Creek Canyon. Below the bridge, the river forms the boundary between the

---

OVERLEAF: *In Tonto National Forest, the Sierra Ancha, one of Arizona's 193 separate mountain ranges, presides over Roosevelt Lake, a recreational paradise that was created by damming the Salt River.*

reservation and the national forest, coursing through a steep canyon of exquisite beauty. It runs about 60 miles before opening into Lake Roosevelt, dropping some 25 feet per mile through more than two dozen rapids. Highly popular, this stretch—though pegged as class III—is hazardous and includes a class V–VI falls. For example, just as the Salt enters Lake Roosevelt, it drops over a 6-foot dam.

From the Salt River Canyon, Route 60 runs through the **Fort Apache Indian Reservation❖,** up the Mogollon Rim to the commercially developed resort areas of Show Low and Pinetop, much-visited spots for camping, fishing, and boating. For a less crowded experience, drop south and then east on Route 73 to Whiteriver, tribal headquarters, and pick up a permit at the office of the tribe's White Mountain Recreation Enterprise, which actively promotes fishing, camping, and hunting bears, pronghorn, and mountain lions in the great pine forests of the reservation. There are many streams and lakes, particularly in the eastern portion. At **Sunrise Lake,** in the northeastern corner, reached by taking Route 260 at Hon Dah to Route 273, is the Sunrise Resort Park, with a hotel, restaurant, and campgrounds. A bit south is the Sunrise Ski Area. Here, at about 9,000 feet, summer nights are cool enough to require a sweater.

The centerpiece of **Mount Baldy Wilderness** is the second-highest peak in the state, at 11,403 feet. A volcano that has been extinct for the last nine million years and was once a much larger lava dome, Mount Bady has been eroded by water—and ice. In Pleistocene times, a glacier gouged out U-shaped canyons, and where the ice could go no farther, dumped rocks in large arcs called terminal moraines. Silt eventually accumulated behind them, creating what are now lovely meadows. Besides the meadows and wide, parklike valleys in the upper reaches (the canyons are typically steep-sided in the lower reaches below the ice), the mountain is thickly forested with Colorado blue spruce (rare in the state), ponderosa pine, white pine, corkbark fir, Engelmann spruce, and aspen. Four river forks originate on its gentle slopes—east and west forks of the Little Colorado, east fork of the White, and west fork of the Black. In the lower portions, elk, mule deer, black bears, and other species thrive. A trail up Mount Baldy begins at Sheep Crossing, reached by a spur road just north of where Route 273 crosses the west fork of the Little Colorado River. The wilderness is within the **Apache-Sitgreaves National Forest❖,** but the peak itself is in the Fort

ABOVE: *Javelinas are wild peccaries that live in bands of 5 to 15 individuals. Vegetarians, they have a special fondness for prickly pear cacti, consuming even the spines.*
LEFT: *The long, sunlit tendrils of ocotillo and plumelike agave flowers sway above a narrow stretch of Salt River Canyon on the Fort Apache Indian Reservation.*

Apache Reservation and is off limits because it is sacred to the Indians. It is enough, however, to hike amid the big boulders (glacial erratics) in the canyons, across the meadows strewn with spring wildflowers, and through the dense woodlands below the peak.

Beyond Sheep Crossing lie two splendid lakes, **Crescent** and **Big,** the latter a 500-acre impoundment considered by many to be the state's premier trout lake, replete with boat rentals, a store, and campgrounds. Beyond, on Route 666 lies the little town of Alpine, a favorite area for cross-country skiers and the jumping-off place for adventuring in the **Blue Range Primitive Area❖.** Here elevations range from 9,000 feet (along the Mogollon Rim) to 5,000 feet in the Blue Range Canyon. The "breaks," sudden changes in elevation, are heavily eroded into small cliffs and outcrops. Elk and white-tailed and mule deer ply the upper elevations, while javelinas, bobcats, and rare kit foxes prowl the lower areas. Among the rare and endangered species of birds are spotted owls, Arizona woodpeckers, and bald eagles.

ABOVE: *With ears designed for both hearing and the dissipation of heat, the kit fox is a relatively common, opportunistic desert carnivore that is monogamously inclined and nervous about coyotes.*

RIGHT: *Corn lily and sneezeweed adorn the Little Colorado River.*

A splendid scenic drive (best accomplished in a high-clearance vehicle) is Forest Road 281, just east of Alpine, along the Blue River to the small community of Blue. About 13 miles along this narrow, well-maintained road is **Upper Blue Campground,** and there is another campground a bit farther. As the road begins to follow the river course, it crosses the Blue several times and runs through the high red cliffs and tall cottonwoods of Jackson Box, where one fords the trickle on a bit of pavement. The road continues a way beyond Blue into land as remote as anyone could want. Just north of Blue, Forest Road 567 winds up the spine of a 12-mile ridge to Route

666, which leads back to Alpine or south out of the Highlands to Clifton.

The wilderness is a paradise for the experienced hiker and backpacker. It is advisable to get a forest service map and consult the ranger in Alpine to select a trail suitable for one's wishes and capabilities. Trails and old forest roads abound, leading from Sonoran woodland to high, riparian forest, through the choppy, vertical breaks, or past huge rock pinnacles, along dancing creeks and silent side canyons. Of one such trail, from KP Cienega to KP Creek, wilderness author David Mazel said: "It is an in-between country, tucked away in a hidden fold between desert and sierra, cactus thorn and pine needle. Here leaves rustle softly in the wind, rather than moan or sigh, and their shadows dance in soothing patterns on the ground. A profound sense of remoteness and intimacy prevails throughout the trip. . . ." The Blue Range Primitive Area, in a word, has it all.

THE PLATEAU: NORTHERN AND EASTERN ARIZONA

The Colorado Plateau is 130,000 square miles of high, mostly flat land that comprises about a third of Arizona, a smaller part of New Mexico, and a section of Utah and Colorado. It has been compared to a serene raft in a surrounding tumultuous sea, a massive piece of geology that somehow managed to keep its head while others around it were losing theirs. For 600 million years, the plateau has remained recognizably itself, while elsewhere great blocks of the earth have been heaved up and compressed, tilting, bending, folding, sinking. It is one of the largest such features on earth.

To be sure, volcanoes have from time to time punched up through the plateau, and the land as a whole has risen over the eons. Rivers as well have carved countless canyons into its richly seamed face, revealing stratum after stratum of rock in the orderly manner by which they were first laid down, one after the other, like the pages of a giant textbook. Here on the plateau, the rocks take on an astonishing array of color. The presence of the iron-bearing minerals hematite or limonite in the original sediment can turn the rock yellow, pink, crimson, even purple and green, depending on the circumstances. Limestone layers may be yellow, gray, or buff. Intermixed are black layers from old lava flows.

LEFT: *It should come as no surprise that such a landscape, at the edge of the Painted Desert on the Navajo Reservation, is known by the Navajo as the dwelling place of spiritual beings called the Holy People.*

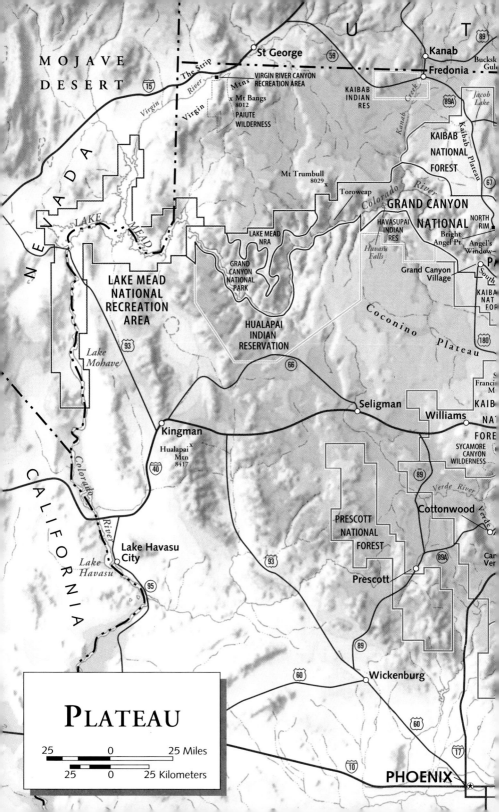

There are badlands of soft rock and clay that swell with each rain, then shrink in the drought, making plant life nearly impossible, and there are highlands covered with dense forest and vast, seemingly limitless expanses of desert grasses. Cliffs of tough sandstone rise above slopes of easily eroded shale. Water and wind sweep away much, exposing, sometimes undercutting cliffs, which crack and tumble down in a chaos of boulders and slabs large and small. Huge wind-carved caves in the faces of cliffs once provided safe neighborhoods for whole villages. Mesas sit like decommissioned battleships on a frozen sea. Every horizon is a phantasmagoria of haunting shape and line, its buttes, pinnacles, notches, nipples all noted carefully by Indians since ancient times as benchmarks to observe the daily motion of the sun in the enormity of the sky, a living calendar explaining when to plant and when to pray.

FLAGSTAFF AND ENVIRONS

The best place to get an introduction to this area is the superb **Museum of Northern Arizona❖,** set in a glade just north of Flagstaff, which is nestled at the base of the great stratovolcano now called San Francisco Peaks. Flagstaff is home to Northern Arizona University, and its ski-minded inhabitants rarely need to pray for snow from October to April; they can glimpse snow on the peaks even in July. The museum's exhibits provide a gentle course in the plateau's geology and natural history, along with numerous insights into the way people such as the Hopi and Navajo have lived as an organic part of this wonderland for centuries. The museum shop is a first-rate place to purchase Native American arts and crafts and load up on books of regional interest, and its superb library of natural history and regional anthropology is open to the public.

Surrounding "Flag" is the single great block of the **Coconino National Forest❖,** in all nearly two million acres, much of it ponderosa country at 6,500–7,500 feet. The most prominent feature of the entire region, visible from hundreds of miles away, is the roughly cone-shaped stratovolcano. The top of the mountain collapsed long ago, and the resulting crater edge eroded into several jagged peaks, four of which bear names. **Humphreys Peak,** at 12,643 feet, is literally the peak of Arizona: One can go no higher in the state.

From here west to Seligman, the plateau is dotted with a dozen old volcanoes and numerous cinder cones, and under a thin layer of soil

Above: *A few rapidly growing plants, including an aspen, pioneer in the Bonito lava flow of Sunset Crater Volcano National Monument east of Flagstaff. The lava here congealed only about 600 years ago.*

the land is covered with basaltic or silicic lava. The westernmost volcanoes were active 15 million years ago; San Francisco Peaks were active from 2.8 million to 200,000 years ago. In the vicinity are some 400 smaller cinder cones, of which the most recent is the namesake of **Sunset Crater Volcano National Monument,** just east of the peaks. This reddish-yellow cone last blew only about 600 years ago, scattering light frothy cinders east and north over an area of more than 800 square miles.

Local people, the Sinagua, fled, presumably in terror, only to find on their return that the cinders conserved soil moisture. A brief population explosion ensued, and several of their stone-slab houses remain a bit north at **Wupatki National Monument❖,** connected to the sunset monument by a highly scenic loop road. Among the many ruins at Wupatki, some not excavated, are the remains of a three-story pueblo with about a hundred rooms, along with an amphitheater and a ball court. Both monuments are pleasant places to hike around and spot abundant wildlife, though Sunset Crater itself, because of its fragility, can no longer be climbed. In the black, rough lava flows around it one can find pio-

neer lichens, and trees have begun to take root in some cinder patches.

San Francisco Peaks, now part of the **Kachina Peaks Wilderness,** were once a single cone some 15,000 feet or more in elevation. In one of its ultimate blasts, the cone blew sideways, creating an interior valley. Much later, glaciers wore down the peaks and smoothed out the valley, leaving rocky moraines across its mouth. The result is called the Inner Basin, now filled with meadows and aspen trees. On the peaks (and in the Grand Canyon) in the 1880s, C. Hart Merriam first noted the succession of life zones now so familiar on these sky islands. At ground level is the ponderosa zone. At 8,000 feet, mixed conifer forest begins; at 9,500 feet, spruce-fir. At 10,500 feet are some subalpine stands of bristlecone pine, those most ancient of trees, and above them is a 1,200-acre island of alpine tundra—the only place it is found in the state. Of the few plants able to grow here, some, such as the San Francisco groundsel, are found nowhere else. Because this alpine ecosystem is so fragile, cross-country hiking is not permitted; one must follow the trail.

Of the several trails to the summit of Humphreys Peak, the most frequented is the eight-mile round-trip on Kachina Peaks Trail, which begins at the Snow Bowl up Forest Road 516 on **Agassiz Peak.** (The face of Agassiz Peak is alive with skiers most of the year, and the ski lift operates in the summer, providing non-hikers with spectacular views west and north. Agassiz has been closed to hiking above the ski area.) The Kachina Peaks Trail leads up to the Humphreys-Agassiz Saddle, and it is a mile farther to the top of this part of the world. The Grand Canyon is visible 75 miles to the north, and to the east the world stretches away across the Painted Desert to the Hopi mesas and beyond. Except for the Hopi reservation, hundreds of square miles of this enormous landscape belong to the nation's largest tribe, the Navajo. Climbing the Peaks in winter through knee-deep snow and occasional gale winds has become popular among the truly robust.

Another reason to step lightly on the upper regions of the Peaks is that this place is deeply sacred for both Navajo and Hopi. The Navajo

LEFT: *Delicate crystals of frost cling to desert plant life in the unforgiving ground of Wupatki National Monument, home to Sinagua ruins.*
OVERLEAF: *Quick to colonize, aspens have taken over an open space in the forest below the summit of San Francisco Peaks, formerly a volcano.*

call it Dok'o'sliid, the western member of the four sacred mountains that delineate their world. For the Hopi, Nuvateekia-ovi is the home of the kachinas, spirits that arrive from winter to summer solstice in the Hopi villages to dance and to bring rain. When not in the villages, the kachinas are on the Peaks, rehearsing. The Hopi, whose priests make periodic pilgrimages to shrines on the Peaks, hope that hikers will do as little as possible to interfere with these rehearsals.

ABOVE: *An uncommon denizen of the mixed coniferous forest, the tassel-eared Abert's squirrel was a new species to nineteenth-century explorer and artist Richard H. Kern.*

RIGHT: *An implosion of asters and gilia blossoms dominates a patch of Sycamore Canyon's bottomlands in the Coconino National Forest.*

Like the forward toes of a bird's foot, three notable canyons have been etched south of Flagstaff, two of them through the lip of the Mogollon Rim. One, eight miles east of the city on Route 40, is found in **Walnut Canyon National Monument❖.** The monument was established to protect the more than 100 Sinagua ruins, dwellings that for the most part were built under the limestone overhangs. A large community thrived here, farming and hunting, from about A.D. 1125 to 1250, then vanished. Why the people left is anyone's guess, but the reasons why they came to this 400-foot-deep canyon are still to be seen and enjoyed by strolling the paved, self-guided trail through the ruins. Aided by volcanic material, the lands on the rim maintained moisture for farming. The canyon's deep meanders and steep sides created a patchwork of sun and shade, an environment that was conducive to a rich flora that in turn attracted game, as well as a wide variety of birds. In addition, there are more than 20 plants that could have been used for medicine and food, including black walnut, wild grape, serviceberry, elderberry, yucca, currant, wild tobacco, and Mormon tea.

South of Flagstaff, Route 89A plummets down **Oak Creek Canyon** in

a spectacular descent from the Mogollon Rim to Sedona. Part of the Coconino National Forest, it may well be the state's second-most-visited canyon, with more than 2.5 million people coming through a year. That may be too crowded for some tastes, but there is a good reason why people throng this 14-mile canyon, chiefly in the summer months: It is exquisitely beautiful. At the northern end, the scenic highway drops almost 800 feet in two miles of dramatic switchbacks, and the canyon grows narrower as it nears Sedona. Along the way are campgrounds, picnic sites, and swimming areas in this perennial creek. About six miles outside Sedona is **Slide Rock State Park❖,** where water stairsteps over smooth, slippery ledges of red sandstone, many of them worn down by the bottoms of children and adults who have, probably since prehistoric times, played otter in this cooling, year-round stream. Along the winding road that crisscrosses the creek are lodges and other facilities, as well as a number of private homes and a hamlet called Indian Gardens. These habitations are mostly hidden in the trees under the towering canyon walls, strange-looking old structures amid the alternating sun and shade, silvery water on rock, and dark pools—all putting one in mind of Oz.

Perhaps the gem of Oak Creek is its **West Fork**, which enters the main creek at milepost 384.5. Although the area is overused by visitors, here towering cliffs and huge rocky overhangs greet the hiker, rocks that seem to have turned into waves; trees growing from vertical rock faces. Lush riparian vegetation, ferns, and improbable flowers fill the canyon where it is wide enough to accommodate anything besides the stream. The hiker crosses the creek numerous times via casual stepping stones. In the first couple of miles the trail is obvious and makes a pleasant day hike and picnic; but the canyon winds on westward for another 12 miles and provides a relatively secluded backpacking trip, with swimming in narrow spots, into a timeless kind of Eden. Numerous other less-crowded trails ranging in difficulty lead from Oak Creek through beautiful areas.

Fifteen miles west is Sycamore Canyon, a 25-mile gash that takes one from plateau country, through the Transition zone, to the Sonoran Desert, where Sycamore Creek merges with the Verde River. While

LEFT: *Little traveled but greatly admired by aficionados of canyon hiking for its variety of habitats and scenic value, Sycamore Canyon in the Coconino National Forest opens out beyond the Packard trailhead.*

most of the approximately 1,000 people who annually hike the entire canyon enter from the south near Clarkdale, one can also start in the north near Whitehorse Lake, south of Williams. The raison d'être for the 56,000-acre **Sycamore Canyon Wilderness❖,** the canyon is in the Coconino, Prescott, and Kaibab National Forests. Toward its southern end are the former habitations of yet other Sinagua communities that housed communes of flower children in the 1960s until the federal government ran them off. The canyon offers rugged hiking among boulders and rocks, high steep cliffs, riparian flora along the creekbed, and magnificent rock formations—the same, in fact, as the upper formations of the Grand Canyon far to the north. Considered one of the state's most scenic backpacking areas, it is not for the faint of heart: One must carry what water will be needed, and among its plentiful wildlife are abundant rattlesnakes, scorpions, and centipedes.

East of Flagstaff, about 35 miles out on Interstate 40, the rim of **Meteor Crater** rises above the plateau 10 miles south. While this is a commercial operation, it is well worth visiting to see the classic type of crater caused by meteorites here and, with much greater frequency, on the moon. Indeed, Apollo astronauts trained here for their lunar hikes. Once known as Coon Bluff, it is 4,000 feet in diameter with a rim that reaches up 160 feet and an interior depression that goes down 600 feet. Hollywood deemed it the fitting setting for the climax of the 1980s movie *Star Man,* although until the late nineteenth century, no one knew that the crater was the result of a meteorite, nor did people believe in such extraterrestrial visitors. A U.S. Geological Survey scientist, G. K. Gilbert, suspected a meteorite because of the thousands of fragments of iron strewn about, most abundant in nearby Canyon Diablo. He investigated, expecting to find magnetic evidence of a huge piece of metal under the crater, but he found none and assumed that the cause was a steam explosion of volcanic origin.

Later a mining engineer, sensing that a half-billion dollars worth of nickel and iron was to be found here, drilled unsuccessfully as late as

RIGHT: *Green enticingly carpets the canyon floor in the Sycamore Canyon Wilderness, along a tough trail south to Valley Verde.*
OVERLEAF: *Pinyon-juniper forest, lit by the late sun, leads up to the edge of the Colorado Plateau's main feature, the Grand Canyon.*

1928. Since then it has been determined that about 25,000 years ago, a 300,000-ton chunk of iron 200 feet in diameter came screaming in slightly faster than an artillery shell, most of it vaporizing on impact. Its youth—it is by far the most recent such impact on earth—and the area's aridity make it the best-preserved crater in the world.

THE GRAND CANYON

North of Flagstaff lies the Destination, the mother of all canyons, whose scenic grandeur has probably caused more film to run through more cameras than any other subject on the planet. It is said that in the early 1500s, when one of Coronado's captains reached the rim of the canyon, he assumed it was a little stream at the bottom of a typical canyon and sent a detail down to fetch water. They returned three days later, bedraggled and exhausted. The Europeans simply had no frame of reference by which to see that it was a big river a full mile below them.

Most first-time visitors to **Grand Canyon National Park❖** see it from the South Rim. After getting over the nearly euphoric shock of viewing such a vista, many note that the North Rim seems higher, and indeed it is. The North Rim consists of a series of plateaus, the highest of which is about 1,200 feet higher than the South Rim's 7,000 feet. Both rims are considered part of a raised plateau, the Kaibab Upwarp. How is it that the Colorado River cut such a magnificent canyon across so elevated a landform? Theories abound. The uplift of the Kaibab plateau probably began 65 million years ago, and a previously popular theory held that the Colorado River, following its present course, began to cut through the gradually uplifting rock about 50 million years ago. The discovery that the Colorado River has run through the canyon for only 5 to 10 million years made that theory untenable. Alternate theories have been proposed and explored through the years. One currently popular theory is an ancient tale of piracy. About 25 million years ago the ancestral Colorado River flowed south out of Utah into Arizona, as now; but confronted by the Upwarp, it turned southward, flowing along the course of the present Little Colorado

RIGHT: *Spencer Terrace, along the Bass Trail on the Grand Canyon's South Rim, provides a typically stunning vista reaching all the way to the North Rim and Kaibab Plateau in Grand Canyon National Park.*

River into a huge lake in eastern Arizona named for the Hopi.

At the same time, waters falling on the western side of the Kaibab Upwarp flowed westward in a complex drainage, and one of these rivers was destined to be a pirate. Its torrential headwaters steadily ate away at the rock, just as other creeks today are doing, creating a canyon that extended farther and farther east, narrowing the rocky divide between the pirate and the Colorado. Eventually the pirate stream broke through the divide, and the torrent of the Colorado took this new and steeper route west. Fed by greatly increased rain and glacial waters from the Rockies, it proceeded to carve out the great canyon we see today. Meanwhile, owing to other conditions, the waters rising far to the east near Mount Baldy began to drain westward into the formerly east-flowing channel of the Little Colorado, scouring out its own impressive gorge and becoming another tributary to the Colorado.

The Grand Canyon is 277 miles long, 18 miles across in places, and at one point 6,200 feet deep. The river has etched out great amphitheaters and coves; erosion has left massive temples with names like Zoroaster and Brahma. The multicolored cliffs, huge buttes, gorges, falls, pools, and tributary creeks beckon one down into its innards to the silver ribbon below, although no one in recorded history had ever run the Colorado until 1869, when John Wesley Powell made his dramatic voyage through its length. Before that, there was even some doubt as to whether the same river entered from the east and exited in the west. Since then, a rich literature about the canyon has accumulated, but Powell's famous account remains for most without peer. Rafting and boating concessionaires (whose waiting lists, by the way, run in years) are fond of quoting Powell along the way. Those who wish to backpack down into the canyon for one or more overnights must also write six months to a year in advance because the Park Service, to protect this heavily used wonder of the world, has had to limit the numbers in the canyon at any given time.

There are plenty of trails into the canyon. The two main ones from the South Rim are **Bright Angel Trail** and **South Kaibab Trail,** each of

LEFT: *This redwall limestone formation takes on a rich glow in the magic sunlight of the fading day here in the inner canyon near Mather Point, on the much-visited South Rim of the Grand Canyon.*

which takes about five hours for the descent and twice that to return to the rim. The two are linked partway down by the **Tonto Trail,** providing a 13-mile loop hike. Descending, one passes layer after layer of differing rock formations, each bespeaking an unimaginable period of time, to the two-billion-year-old rock (dark schist and gneiss) on the bottom. One also goes through the three classic life zones—a Transition zone of ponderosa; below that, at 6,500 feet, the Upper Sonoran zone, with pinyon and juniper; and from 4,000 feet to the bottom, the Lower Sonoran zone of yucca and sagebrush. Over on the upper elevations of the North Rim are Canadian zone spruce and fir. Thus by descending the canyon one can walk through two billion years of geological history and through the vegetative equivalent of a hike from the Mexican border to British Columbia. Be advised that to go to the bottom and back is an overnight trip; but be further advised that a night in the canyon's depths—gazing up at the moon or the stars hanging above, somehow all the more mysterious when defined by the canyon walls, or watching tendrils of light probe the sky at dawn—is an experience that can render poets mute.

ABOVE: *However unimpressed this egg-laden female collared lizard appears by her grand surroundings, she is a feisty character with a strong, quick bite, often found lurking along limestone ledges.*

RIGHT: *Along the Grand Canyon's Lower Hermit Trail, a western redbud tree bursts into glorious spring flower.*

Trekker David Mazel recommends a three-mile (round-trip) day trip from Yaki Point to Cedar Ridge—basically the upper part of the **South Kaibab Trail**—to experience being about 1,000 feet down in the canyon without spending all day on the trail. The hike offers splendid vistas of Zoroaster and Brahma temples east across the canyon and of Pipe Creek Canyon to the west. Walking the length of the **Rim Trail** offers one unsurpassed views, as does taking any of the several scenic drives and stopping off at the overlooks. Not to be missed is the magnificent **Havasu Falls,** located along Havasu Creek in the western part of the canyon. A 12-mile hike leads to a well-managed and controlled streamside campground

with three beautiful, crystalline blue-green waterfalls and pools. This is, by far, one of the most idyllic spots in the world. The visitor center, museum, and amphitheater in **Grand Canyon Village** provide excellent background material for people who want to engage in any of the myriad activities available—ranging from the strenuous to the relaxed. However one enjoys the canyon, it is a must.

NAVAJO COUNTRY

East of the Grand Canyon, the forbidding realm of the Painted Desert stretches away in a southeastward sweep all the way to Holbrook and beyond, mostly spreading out along the course of the Little Colorado River. The river itself is almost always bone dry, but a river beneath it, flowing through underground sand and gravel, carries plenty of water for the cottonwoods that grow on its banks. Beyond are badlands of a wild palette; the barren, hilly land, broken occasionally by a rocky ledge or outcrop, is variously blue, white, gray, dark red, green, and yellow—and altogether otherworldly. Almost washed out at midday, the badlands glow richly when the sun is low in the sky.

These badlands consist mostly of sand, clay, and river- and shale-deposited sandstone—a feature called the Chinle Formation. Rare torrential rains cause the clay to swell, and then it dries into a flaky crust that the winds carry off, making it almost impossible for plants to establish themselves. Here and there, some hardy grasses eke out a living. But the land was not always so. Fossils of ferns, freshwater fish, and snails, along with early dinosaurs, suggest that this region was once mostly swamps, languid rivers, lagoons, and tropical forest, a place of much stagnant water. Under such circumstances (where there is little oxygen present as plants decay underwater), the iron content of the clay produces the bizarre colors now seen.

The vast proportion of the Painted Desert is in the Navajo Reservation; but some 50,000 acres of it, called the **Painted Desert Wilderness,** are within the **Petrified Forest National Park**❖, 25 miles east of Holbrook and north of

ABOVE: *In this hurried but exquisite turn-of-the-century sketch in pencil, watercolor, and gouache, artist Thomas Moran looked up the trail at Bright Angel Point.*

LEFT: *One of the earliest Anglo visitors to the Grand Canyon, Moran (photographed at work by William Henry Jackson in 1892) brought unimagined vistas of the West back to a manifestly adoring eastern public.*

OVERLEAF: *The eroded clayey configurations of the Chinle Formation in the Painted Desert near Ives Mesa respond with eerie stripes to the late afternoon sun.*

233

ABOVE: *The scarlet blossoms of Indian paintbrush thrive in a former swampland.*

RIGHT: *About 225 million years ago, coniferous trees fell in a swamp, sank into anaerobic waters, and turned to rock; now they are the extraordinary centerpieces of Petrified Forest National Park.*

Interstate 40. This area, and half of the park south of the highway, seem from the road to be little but flat, waterless, mountainless, canyonless, hot badlands. True enough, but beginning 225 million years ago, this was a great, damp forest of huge conifers related to trees called *Araucarias,* which thrive today in the Southern Hemisphere. As they fell, the trees were washed downstream and buried in the silt and oxygen-free water so they could not decompose as a rotting log does. Instead, the silica-rich water bathed them in minerals that invaded their cells, converting them to precise stone versions of the living things they had been—petrified wood.

A visitor center and other facilities are north of the interstate, and beyond a road leads onto an escarpment that overlooks the astounding lunarscape of the Painted Desert close at hand. At Kachina Point, there is a museum, formerly an inn, and a trailhead pointing down into Lithodendron Wash. The trail peters out to leave the hiker entirely on his or her own in a realm formed so long ago and today informed by a silence so complete that one's heartbeat may be the loudest sound. People (with a permit) who have spent the night out under the stars among these desolate hills feel as though they have returned from another part of the solar system.

Beyond Kachina Point, near **Chinle Point,** paleontologists in 1984 discovered what appears to be the oldest known dinosaur, a German shepherd–sized, plant-eating plateosaur some 225 million years old that may have been the ancestor of the brontosaurs. From here, the road loops south across the interstate and the Santa Fe Railroad tracks, past the Puerco Ruin, an Anasazi dwelling reached via a paved path accessi-

ABOVE: *Drawing nourishment from the inhospitable clay-based soil of the Painted Desert, a rabbitbrush manages an ebullient moment under a characteristically changeable southwestern summer sky.*

ble by wheelchair. A turnout leads to **Newspaper Rock,** what amounts to an Anasazi bulletin board of petroglyphs, some of which may have played a calendrical role. On the summer solstice visitors can watch several Anasazi calendars (wells) filled precisely by the beams of sunrise.

Beyond lies **Blue Mesa,** where a turnout provides a view of low outlandish hills called haystacks, striped in various colors from top to bottom. **Agate Bridge** is just that, a more-than-100-foot long log that turned to agate; its ends, embedded in resistant ground, were undercut by a 40-foot ravine. Beyond, in Jasper Forest, Crystal Forest, **Long Logs Trail,** and Rainbow Forest are the finest assemblages of petrified wood in the world. Along Long Logs Trail is a unique pueblo, partially restored: It was made entirely of pieces of petrified wood.

Before Teddy Roosevelt made this a national monument, and even thereafter, souvenir collectors and merchants made a practice of taking pieces of this old forest home with them. In their multicolored mystery, they pose the same temptation today, an urge that is to be severely sublimated.

What the Grand Canyon offers in utter splendor, some say Canyon de Chelly can claim in sheer beauty. Pronounced "de Shay," it is a national monument of the same name in the heart of the Navajo

ABOVE: *A rare summer flood cascades over Grant Falls on the Little Colorado River, normally a dry wash lined with scraggly cottonwoods and once a more significant tributary to the Colorado.*

Reservation. To get there from Holbrook is to travel one of the most unheralded and wonderfully lonely scenic routes in the state, up Route 77 through Navajoland. Great plains sweep away to lonely mesas and buttes, against which one sees typical Navajo homesteads—a traditional house, an octagonal building called a hogan (accent the last syllable); a shade house made of tree poles; and a corral for sheep, cattle, or horses. Distantly, one may spy the sheep themselves, tended by a youth, or an old Navajo woman in a velvet shirt and long skirt, or perhaps merely a Navajo sheepdog. Except for a pickup or two, this is how it has been for centuries, a life so quiet that the loudest sound is usually the bellwether sheep on the way home.

A few miles beyond Indian Wells, Route 15 leads through more of the same, crossing Route 264 and as Route 63, sweeping into the aptly named Beautiful Valley on the way to the town of Chinle and **Canyon de Chelly National Monument❖.** The monument consists of one main canyon—Canyon de Chelly, with **Canyon del Muerto, Mon-**

OVERLEAF: *Near Ward Terrace in the Navajo Indian Reservation, the spring winds howl with biting dust over the eroded rocks of the Chinle Formation, continually shaping its natural sculpture.*

ument Canyon, and the much smaller **Black Rock Canyon** feeding off it. One can be standing on the red rimrock, where potholes scoured out by the wind hold water briefly after a rain, and be unaware that there is a thousand-foot drop only a few feet away. From such a vantage point the world looks all of a piece, stretching away to misty blue shapes on the horizon, the looming Chuska Mountains to the east, the brow of Black Mesa to the west, and the godlit pinnacles of Monument Valley distantly to the northwest. Then, abruptly, the world falls dizzyingly away, revealing precipitous red, brown, and peach walls of sandstone, a seemingly lazy river making its sandy way far below along the canyon floor, with the vibrant green of cottonwoods and tamarisks honoring its passage. Here and there appears a storybook orchard, a residence for a Navajo family, and in the walls, in huge caverns swept out by wind, dust, and water, the rectangular ruins of Anasazi dwellings. Here in 1864 Kit Carson was sent to "round up" the Navajo and deport them from their lands to a distant internment camp in eastern New Mexico—the lamentable Long Walk.

There are two rim drives with turnouts overlooking various parts of the canyons, and one may walk down to **White House Ruin,** a round-trip hike of 2.5 miles. Beyond the White House Ruin trailhead at the rim, approximately 12.5 miles up the canyon on South Rim Drive, one sees an extraordinary pinnacle, standing alone and seeming to reach nearly as high as the canyon rim. This is Spider Rock, one of the Navajo's most sacred areas. It is the home of Spider Woman, a principal figure in the Navajo's Creation Stories, who among other things taught the Navajo how to weave.

Intermittent beds of the sandstone walls of Canyon de Chelly show the canyon's bottom level at different times, and the cross bedding indicates sand dune movement some 200 to 280 million years ago. This formation suggests that the area was once part of a great sea that receded, leaving fine sedimented sandstone that gradually broke down to sand. The resulting sand dunes were transported by the high winds and water movements of the time. According to some theorists, the formation also

---

LEFT: *Cottonwoods turn a golden yellow along the perpetual stream that meanders over quicksand a thousand feet down on the floor of Canyon de Chelly, a storied place of Navajo resistance in the 1860s.*

suggests that this was part of a larger mega-continent often called Pangaea, and that it was situated in the vicinity of our present equator.

The best way to see the canyon is from the bottom, but because safety is a concern and because it is the Navajo's home, one must be accompanied by a park ranger or a Navajo guide, which can be arranged at the visitor center. Concessioners offer horseback riding into the canyon, and Thunderbird Lodge, inside the monument, runs occasional four-wheel-drive-vehicle tours. Much of the creek bed is quicksand, and numerous vehicles have simply had to be abandoned as they sank out of sight—puzzles for future archaeologists to sort out.

A lovely departure is from the North Rim, Route 64, along the edge of Canyon del Muerto to Tsaile, the main campus of the Navajo Community College, a remarkable building that rises out of the surrounding conifers. Route 12 leads through the Chuska Mountains, south past Wheatfields Lake and heartbreakingly beautiful red rock formations, eventually to Window Rock, headquarters for the Navajo Nation.

Or one can go north from Chinle to Many Farms and take Route 59 to Kayenta and thence to the quintessential rock formation of the entire Southwest—**Monument Valley❖.** These dramatic spires and buttes have been made familiar to virtually everyone in the country by John Wayne's western movies and by many automobile commercials in which new models are shown dramatically perched on one or another flat-topped pillar. (The trick, by the way, is to take only the shell of the new model up by helicopter, photograph it in the late afternoon, then take it down, alter it into yet another model, and repeat the process the next day.)

These stunning formations have been produced by erosion. The spires, mesas, and buttes came into being as running water, rock falls, and slow weathering etched away the softer shale around the bases. Great vertically fractured slabs fell away from the massive sandstone buttes and pillars.

For a modest fee, one can drive the tour road through the monument or arrange for a guided tour. To spend the night in the campground on a promontory high above the valley, watching these eerie towers in the

RIGHT: *One of several Anasazi ruins in Canyon de Chelly National Monument, Mummy Cave broods over Canyon del Muerto, where many Navajos died at the hands of Kit Carson's troops in the 1860s.*

ABOVE: *From Hunt's Mesa, the spires and pinnacles of Monument Valley beckon on the horizon. Once a vast area of sand dunes that*

moonlight and at dawn, is tantamount to a mystical experience.

Near Monument Valley is a far less well known place of nearly equivalent magic. **Mystery Valley,** whose whereabouts are not noted on maps or guides lest it be overrun, is considered a part of Monument Valley by the Navajo, who call them both by one name, Tse' Bii Ndzisgaii. It hosted small Anasazi homesites up to about 600 years ago, some single room structures of stone, many in excellent states of preservation. Never did more than 30 people live here at a time, making it a remote backwater of the grand and widespread Anasazi culture. Other ruins attest to a subsequent time when Navajo lived in the valley. It has been called an "enormous geological soufflé" with rounded wind sculptures and swirling patterns in the rock formed by old solidified dunes rising as high as 100 feet above the valley floor, narrow canyons, big wind-carved caves where the ancient people built homes, and rows of smaller holes. Many of the walls are dotted with pictographs—human

246

hardened into rock called the de Chelly formation, the eerie shapes are among the most well known products of erosion in the world.

hands, human figures, clearly identifiable pronghorns, bighorn sheep.

To visit this mysterious place, it is necessary to book a Navajo-guided tour between April and October at Goulding Trading Post and Lodge, north of Kayenta and near Monument Valley.

Just south of Tuba City and the outlying Hopi village of Moenkopi is one of the less known and more astounding canyons in the state, **Coal Canyon.** Remote and silent, this sizable gash in the earth sports colors, mostly reds, yellows, and whites, that are of a primary purity unparalleled by most better-known and more frequented canyons. Ten miles west of Tuba City Route 160 meets Route 89, and a few miles north of that juncture a sign points out an area off the road where, more than 70 million years ago, a host of dinosaurs left their footprints in soft earth that eventually hardened into stone. To the north lies Page, the Glen Canyon Dam, and 186-mile-long Lake Powell, which fills up several once beautiful lakes and is the centerpiece of the **Glen Canyon**

National Recreation Area❖, highly popular with boaters (particularly on the Utah side). The Navajo tribe is planning to build a resort hotel on the Arizona shore of the lake. Better to turn west across Navajo Bridge, just south of Page, and head for the untrammeled lands of the Strip.

STRIP COUNTRY

The northwest corner of Arizona, called the Strip, is 11,000 square miles of lonely open space that is home to about 3,000 people. For many years, the only vehicular crossing of the Colorado River in the state was Lees Ferry in Marble Canyon, where the river widens and slows (a few miles north of where Navajo Bridge is now). The strip was so remote that residents of the now-defunct town of Mount Trumbull had to drive nearly 300 miles—through three states—to get to Kingman, their Mojave County county seat. Separated culturally as well as geographically from the rest of Arizona, most of the inhabitants are descended from Mormon colonists, and most go to Utah to shop. The vast proportion of the area is public land held by the Bureau of Land Management, though of course here as well is the North Rim of **Grand Canyon National Park** and a sizable chunk of national forest.

The Strip is a series of plateaus, with the **Kaibab Plateau** rising to an elevation of about 9,000 feet, well above the Paria Plateau to the east and the Kanab to the west. The Uinkaret is slightly higher than the Kanab, while the Shivwits in the west is some 2,500 feet above sea level near the river. Not surprisingly, with such a range in elevation, there is desert—Mojave Desert with Joshua trees and barrel cacti—in the west and Hudsonian spruce-fir forests on the Kaibab Plateau's upper reaches. The ponderosa forests of the Kaibab Plateau are the only home of the Kaibab squirrel, a perky and often seen gray creature with tufted ears and an almost transparent tail.

Most visitors to the Strip are headed for the North Rim of the Grand Canyon for hiking, camping, or mule trips, and many are content to view this spectacular arena from **Bright Angel Point** or to drive the Cape Royal Road to the Walhalla Overlook and prowl around **Angel's**

RIGHT: *Monument Valley, a Navajo tribal park, glows as dusk nears. Camping on a promontory overlooking the moonlit spires and strange formations is, for many, a profoundly moving experience.*

Window, a massive natural bridge on the canyon's edge. About 400,000 people visit the North Rim annually (one tenth the amount that visit the South Rim), but their stays tend to be longer. The park closes from October to April when the plateau receives some 120 inches of snow: A growing number of winter campers cross-country ski to the rim.

Whether headed for the park or some more remote area, the visitor crossing Navajo Bridge is greeted by the **Vermilion Cliffs,** a massive and magnificent formation of steep sandstone cliffs with rounded edges that rises from 1,000 feet above the highway, Route 89A, in the eastern end to 3,000 feet in the western end. The cliffs and nearby Paria Canyon and a good deal of land in between compose the 110,000-acre **Paria Canyon–Vermilion Cliffs Wilderness❖.**

Paria Canyon twists down out of Utah, emerging at Lees Ferry, no longer a ferry but a popular place to put in for a run down the Colorado. Most people bent on trekking Paria Canyon's entire 35-mile length (a trip of four or five days) begin at the White House Trailhead in Utah. About 4 miles in are the Narrows, where the canyon is about 50 feet wide and the walls tower 1,500 feet up. For 5 miles there is no way to escape flash floods, which are common from July to September. Visitors starting at the Lees Ferry Trailhead find that their weather information is dated by the time they reach the Narrows. Many make day hikes partway upstream from this trailhead.

It is a rugged trip through spectacular country, but even more spectacular (and scary) is to start the trek at Wire Pass Trailhead into Buckskin Gulch, which intersects Paria Canyon after a 12-mile hike through a canyon so narrow that its overhangs often obscure the sky altogether. At one point, called The Dive, it is a mere 3 feet wide. Flash floods are truly a hazard here in what has been called a "natural storm drain," with some floods reaching depths of 20 feet and more. The bureau's hiker's guide to Paria Canyon is adorned with a drawing of the narrow canyon with a huge log stuck between its walls some 30 feet above the floor.

Route 89A turns north in House Rock Valley, home of a bison herd that is occasionally seen from the road, and then climbs up onto Kaibab

---

LEFT: *Lit by the radiant sun and dusted by a spring snow, fancifully named Buddha Temple rises up against the high North Rim of the Grand Canyon, as the Tonto Plateau lies deep in shadow below.*

Plateau, often called "an island in the sky." The plateau receives far more precipitation than its surround and is poorly drained by streams. Instead, water percolates down through passageways that have been dissolved out of the underlying limestone. The grandiosely named Jacob's Lake is a sinkhole caused when one of these passageways collapsed. Routes 89A and 67 pass through the northern block of the **Kaibab National Forest❖,** much overlooked as a place for hiking through cool forests (40–70 degrees fahrenheit in summer) and meadows painted with wildflowers. At one time it provided a classic case of game mismanagement. President Theodore Roosevelt made it a game refuge around the turn of the century; deer hunting was prohibited, but predators were fair game. The result was a population explosion among the deer and such serious overbrowsing that the deer population crashed. Hunting is now carefully controlled and the vegetation has largely replenished itself. The beginning segment of the Arizona Trail, called Kaibab Plateau Trail, starts in the forest and weaves its way through outstanding scenery. The trail eventually makes its way to the Mexican border, crossing through four national forests and one national park.

The western boundary of the Kaibab Plateau is formed by Kanab Creek, a major tributary to the Colorado. From its headwaters in Utah, Kanab Creek runs 57 miles south, cutting into the Kanab and Kaibab plateaus to form **Kanab Canyon.** With walls as high as 1,000 feet and a floor often as narrow as 40 feet, this is another rugged trek for the experienced backpacker. On his second Colorado River expedition, John Wesley Powell pulled his battered boats out where Kanab Creek meets the river and fought his way up the canyon on horseback, often having to lead the animals over and around the boulders strewn about the floor and along precipitous ledges. The trip is somewhat easier on foot and descending—overall a drop of some 2,500 feet—but this, too, is a difficult journey and particularly in the summer flash-flood season, a dangerous one. The creek's upper reaches pass through the Kaibab Paiute Indian Reservation; it then descends into **Kanab Creek Wilderness,** which is jointly managed by the Kaibab National Forest and the Bureau of Land Management, before finally entering Grand Canyon National Park. Permits are required for the portion inside the park. For those up to it, Kanab Creek Wilderness has been described as sublime.

In the very northwestern corner of the state loom the **Virgin**

ABOVE: *In the rugged and sublime Kanab Creek Wilderness, the moon rises over Hack Canyon, a side canyon to the major gorge, cut by Kanab Creek, which then leads into the Grand Canyon from the north.*

Mountains. Located in the **Paiute Wilderness,** they rise precipitously a mile above the Mojave Desert on their western slope, and the summit of their highest peak, Mount Bangs (8,012 feet), is 6,300 feet above the beautiful Virgin River, which winds along their northern flanks. Mount Bangs can be climbed in a day from a parking area near Cougar Spring in the southern end of the wilderness, a 1,700-foot ascent compared to climbing up out of the Grand Canyon. From this same trailhead, one can take the strenuous Virgin Ridge Loop along the sharp backbone ridge of these rugged and unforgiving mountains. At the northern end is a Bureau of Land Management campground, the **Virgin River Canyon Recreation Area❖,** from which a pleasant day hike takes one along the river to Migrant's Cove and back. The hardy may wish to follow in the footsteps of famed mountain man Jedediah Smith, who, as early as 1826, walked from Migrant's Cove into Sullivan's Canyon, along the

253

course of the Virgin River, south out of the mountains.

Here is a splendid isolation. Use of the wilderness is estimated to average about one party per day, including picnickers and white-water rafters on the Virgin River.

Nine miles west of Fredonia on Route 389, a dirt road turns off to the south and runs along east of Bull Rush Canyon through flat desertland. Ahead on the horizon, **Mount Trumbull❖** looms, the highest point in the area at 8,029 feet and a Bureau of Land Management Wilderness Area. In the last century the area around the mountain was timbered by Mormons (for a temple in St. George, Utah), but not its summit. One may hike to the top of this basalt-capped sky island, among undisturbed stands of stately ponderosas, and look out across the lonely terrain of the Strip. Or one can continue south into a largely undeveloped portion of Grand Canyon National Park, past the Tuweep Ranger Station to the canyon overlook called **Toroweap❖.** Here are huge boulders and slabs to perch on, and ancient lava spills draped over the North Rim. There is little but the sound of the wind and of water tumbling 30 feet over Lava Falls a sheer drop of 3,000 feet below, the tiered colors of the canyon stretch away for miles and miles, and below, a great volcanic neck punches up right out of the Colorado. It is called Vulcan's Throne, a proper evocation of the gods of a heroic era. Many consider this overlook the most spectacular view of the most spectacular natural feature on the continent, what writer Douglas Chadwick has called "an unmistakable call for prayer."

This grandest of canyons is a long way, and a far cry, from the rolling Kiowa grasslands, the searing heat of the Jornada del Muerto, the cool, dark, and fantastic forms of Carlsbad Caverns, the stately saguaro sentinels of the Sonoran Desert. And standing here, or in many of the places along the various routes through the Southwest, one can be forgiven for imagining what people here have long imagined. They have spun myths, creation stories, songs to unseen deities. They have meditated on the fierce beauty around them and felt part of it. They have said, "This is where the world begins."

LEFT: *The Colorado River courses with ancient dignity 3,000 feet below Toroweap overlook on the Grand Canyon's North Rim.*

OVERLEAF: *Under lowering skies, the setting sun intensifies the reds of Sedona's rocks, as it highlights the ridges of the towering Mogollon Rim.*

FURTHER READING ABOUT THE SOUTHWEST

ABBEY, EDWARD. *The Monkey Wrench Gang*. 1975. Reprint, New York: Avon, 1992. This outrageous novel is a wondrously anarchic tour through the Arizona landscape and mindscape.

ACKERMAN, DIANE. *Twilight of the Tenderfoot: A Western Memoir.* New York: Morrow, 1980. Acclaimed nature writer's account of time spent on a New Mexico ranch, with additional musings about regional poets and writers.

CATHER, WILLA. *Death Comes for the Archbishop*. 1927. Reprint, New York: Vintage, 1990. The feel of New Mexico—its light, sky, and meaning—is nowhere better expressed than in this classic novel based on the life of Archbishop Lamy of Santa Fe.

CHRONIC, HALKA. *The Roadside Geology of New Mexico.* Edited by David Alt and Donald Hyndman. Missoula, MT: Mountain Press, 1987. A good addition to any glove compartment, this geologic highway guide written for the nonscientist details the ancient marvels still to be seen—even from a car window (with maps).

ELDREDGE, CHARLES C., Julie Schimmel, and William H. Truettner. *Art in New Mexico, 1900-1945: Paths to Taos and Santa Fe.* New York: Abbeville, 1986. Lavishly illustrated survey of two generations of American artists who found their great inspiration in the life, land, and light of New Mexico.

GILBERT, BILL. *Westering Man: The Life of Joseph Walker.* New York: Atheneum, 1983. For a sense of the land when it was pristine, this biography is a classic account of the greatest of all mountain men.

HILLERMAN, TONY. *Dance Hall of the Dead.* New York: HarperCollins, 1973. A fictional tour de force that provides fine insight into Indian country, particularly Navajoland. Winner of the Edgar Allan Poe award as best mystery of the year.

———. *New Mexico, Rio Grande and Other Essays.* Portland,OR: Graphic Arts Center, 1992. Essays and photographs that celebrate New Mexico, the great rivers of the Southwest, and the Native American perspective on the sanctity of the earth.

MacMAHON, JAMES A. *Deserts. The Audubon Society Nature Guide.* New York: Knopf, 1985. This fully illustrated field guide (with descriptions of flora, fauna, and rocks) is a superb introduction to the Southwest's four desert types.

MILLER, TOM, ed. *Arizona: The Land and the People.* Tucson: University of Arizona Press, 1986. Whimsical portraits of the state's regions and peoples woven together by a series of vignettes set "off the beaten track."

PAGE, JAKE, and SUSANNE PAGE. *Hopi.* Bergenfield, NJ: Abrams, 1982. Listed as one of the 100 best books about Arizona by the governor's office, this gorgeously photographed volume sets Hopi life into the context of the state's natural and spiritual surroundings.

PARENT, LAWRENCE. *The Hiker's Guide to New Mexico.* Helena, MT: Falcon Press, 1994. A comprehensive guide to more than 70 hikes, including maps, charts, photos, and detailed descriptions covering the degree of difficulty of each hike, its location, length, elevation, best season, water availability, and more.

POWELL, JOHN WESLEY. *The Exploration of the Colorado River and its Canyons.* New York: Penguin Books Nature Library, 1987. Nothing can beat this first-person account, first published in 1895, of the last great piece of discovery on this continent.

SMITH, DEAN, ed. *Arizona Highways Album: The Road to Statehood.* Phoenix: Arizona Department of Transportation, 1987. Vintage photographs evocatively recall life in Arizona before 1912 as well as the years that followed.

WHITNEY, STEPHEN. *A Field Guide to the Grand Canyon.* New York: Quill, 1982. An excellent one-volume guide to America's greatest natural wonder—useful, in fact, for exploring virtually any southwestern canyon.

ABOVE: *For Americans, the lure of the West has always been more powerful than the considerable travails of cross-country travel. The road did dead-end spectacularly, however, for this 1902 Arizona tourist.*

GLOSSARY

Spanish words appear in roman type.

agave century plant, a member of the amaryllis family having spiny-margined leaves; some are cultivated for their fiber or for ornament

alluvial fan deposit of alluvium: gravel, sand, and smaller materials that have formed a fan shape, usually at the base of mountains; created by water rushing down a mountain

aquifer underground layer of porous water-bearing rock, sand, or gravel.

barchan crescent-shaped sand dune

batholith large mass of igneous rock that has melted into surrounding strata and lies a great distance below the earth's surface

boreal relating to the northern biotic area characterized especially by dominance of coniferous forests

bosque "thicket" or "woods" in Spanish

butte tall, steep-sided tower of rock formed from an eroded plateau; buttes delay inevitable erosional changes because of their hard uppermost layer of rock

caldera crater with a diameter many times that of the vent, formed by collapse of a volcano's center

chaparral dense thicket of shrubs or dwarf trees; an ecological community consisting of shrubby plants especially adapted to dry summers and moist winters

cholla any of several very spiny, many branched cacti

cicncga marshland

cinder cone cone-shaped hill formed from the accumulation of charred lava that builds up around the vent of a volcano

climax species species that has reached the hypothetical condition of stability in which all successional changes in the community have taken place; further changes only follow destructive disturbances

cuesta hill or ridge with a steep face on one side and a gentle slope on the other

ephemeral plant that flowers for a very short time, even an hour or less

fault block mountain characterized by steep walls on one side and gentler slopes on the other; formed when plate movement causes land on one side of the fault to rise higher than on the other side

glacial erratic rock or boulder transported from its original resting place by a glacier

gneiss foliated metamorphic rock similar in composition to granite or other feldspathetic plutonic rock

grama grassland area characterized by dense tufts or mats of grasses of the genus *Bouteloua;* often used as pasture; found in western North America and in South America

hoodoo natural column of rock often formed into fantastic shapes; found in western North America

kiva ceremonial structure, usually underground, used by Pueblo Indians

lava tube tunnel formed when the upper crust of a lava flow cools and solidifies, and the molten lava below flows out

lek assembly area where birds and especially prairie chickens carry on courtship behavior

magma molten rock material within the earth that becomes an igneous rock when it cools

mesa isolated, relatively flat-topped natural elevation more extensive than a butte and less extensive than a plateau

mesic characterized by or relating to a moderate amount of moisture

mestizo persons of mixed Indian and Spanish ancestry

montane relating to the biogeographic zone of relatively moist, cool upland slopes below timberline; dominated by evergreen trees

petroglyph carving or drawing on rock, especially one made by prehistoric people

playa flat-floored bottom of an undrained desert basin that may become a shallow lake at times

quartzite compact granular rock composed of quartz and formed from the metamorphism of quartz sandstone

rapids broken, fast-flowing water that tumbles around boulders; classified from I to VI according to increasing difficulty of watercraft navigation

rift valley long, thin valley with steep sides formed when plate movement splits the earth's crust

riparian relating to the bank of a natural watercourse, lake, or tidewater

sagebrush North American hoary composite subshrub; has a bitter juice and an odor resembling sage; found on alkaline plains throughout western U.S.

saguaro treelike cactus of the southwestern desert region; bears white flowers and edible fruit

schist metamorphic rock with a layered appearance; composed of often flaky parallel layers of chiefly micaceous minerals

sinkhole funnel-shaped hole formed where water has collected in the cracks of limestone, dissolved the rock, and carried it away; also formed when roofs of caves collapse

spatter cone cone-shaped formation made of ejected clots of lava built up on the vent of a volcano

spelunker one who studies and explores caves

stromatolite fossil formed from the trapping of sediment by layers of blue-green algae

talus rock debris that accumulates at the base of a cliff

terminal moraine heap of mixed rock debris, carried and deposited by a glacier, that marks the farthest advance of the ice

trade wind wind blowing almost constantly in one direction

travertine mineral formed by deposition from spring waters or hot springs, forming (among other deposits) stalactites and stalagmites

vaquero herdsman, cowboy

volcanic tuff rock formed by an ash flow

wash dry bed of a stream

yucca evergreen plant of genus *Yucca*, often having a tall stout stem and a terminal cluster of white flowers; native to warmer regions of North America

LAND MANAGEMENT RESOURCES

The following public and private organizations are among the important administrators of the preserved and protected areas described in this volume. Brief explanations of the various legal and legislative designations of these areas follow.

MANAGING ORGANIZATIONS

Arizona State Parks
State agency responsible for administration and maintenance of all state parks, public lands and historic sites.

Arizona Game and Fish Department
Agency responsible for conservation and administration of state wildlife resources; maintains state hunting and fishing areas and licenses

Bureau of Land Management (BLM) Department of the Interior
Administers nearly half of all federal lands, some 272 million acres. Resources are managed for multiple uses: recreation, grazing, logging, mining, fish and wildlife, and watershed and wilderness preservation.

National Park Service (NPS) Department of the Interior
Regulates the public's use of national parks, monuments, and preserves. Resources are managed to protect landscape, natural and historic artifacts, and wildlife. Administers historic and natural landmarks, national seashores, wild and scenic rivers, and the national trail system.

The Nature Conservancy (TNC) Private organization
International nonprofit organization that owns the largest private system of nature sanctuaries in the world, some 1,300 preserves. Its aim is to preserve significant and diverse plants, animals, and natural communities. Some areas are managed by other private or public groups, some by the Conservancy.

New Mexico Department of Energy, Minerals, and Natural Resources
State agency that oversees all 37 state parks and administers all state forests, rangelands, soil, and water resources.

U.S. Fish and Wildlife Service (USFWS) Department of the Interior
Principal govermental agency responsible for conserving, protecting, and enhancing the country's fish and wildlife and their habitats. Manages national wildlife refuges and fish hatcheries as well as programs for migratory birds and endangered and threatened species.

U.S. Forest Service (USFS) Department of Agriculture
Administers more than 190 million acres in the national forests and national grasslands and is responsible for the management of their resources. Determines how best to combine commercial uses such as grazing, mining, and logging with conservation needs.

DESIGNATIONS

Area of Critical Environmental Concern
Land designated under the authority of the 1976 federal Land Policy and

Management Act where expert management is needed to protect a sensitive natural area. Managed by the BLM.

National Conservation Area

Special area to be used for recreation or other specific purposes set aside by Congress to protect specific environments. Managed by the BLM.

National Forest

Large acreage managed for the use of forests, watersheds, wildlife, and recreation by both the public and private companies and individuals. Managed by the USFS.

National Historic Site

Land area, building, or object preserved because of its national historic importance. Managed by the NPS.

National Monument

Nationally significant landmark, structure, or object; or an area of scientific or historic importance. Managed by the NPS.

National Natural Landmark

Nationally significant natural area that is a prime example of a biotic community or a particular geological feature. Managed by the NPS.

National Park

Spacious primitive or wilderness land area that contains scenery and natural wonders so outstanding that it has been preserved by the federal government. Managed by the NPS.

National Recreation Area

Site established to conserve and develop for recreational purposes an area of national scenic, natural, or historic interest. Power boats, dirt and mountain bikes, and ORVs allowed with restrictions. Managed by the NPS.

National Wildlife Refuge

Public land set aside for wild animals; refuges protect migratory waterfowl, help preserve endangered and threatened species, and provide a secure habitat for native plants. Managed by USFW.

Reservation

Area of land held in trust by the federal government and reserved for use by native Americans.

Wild and Scenic River System

National program set up to preserve selected rivers in their natural free-flowing condition (they must have an outstanding scenic, recreational, geologic, wildlife, historic, or archaeologic feature) as well as to develop other rivers for hydropower purposes. Management shared by BLM, NPS, and USFW.

Wilderness Area

Area with particular ecological, geological, or scientific, scenic, or historic value that has been set aside in its natural condition to be preserved as wild land; limited recreational use is permitted. Managed by the BLM.

NATURE TRAVEL

The following is a selection of national and local organizations that sponsor nature-related travel activities from extended tours to day trips and ecology workshops

NATIONAL

National Audubon Society
700 Broadway
New York, NY 10003
(212) 979-3000
Offers a wide range of ecological field studies, tours, and cruises throughout the United States

National Wildlife Federation
1400 16th St. NW
Washington, D.C. 20036
(703) 790-4363
Offers training in environmental education for all ages, wildlife camp and teen adventures, conservation summits involving nature walks, field trips, and classes

The Nature Conservancy
1815 North Lynn St.
Arlington, VA 22209
(703) 841-5300
Offers a variety of excursions from regional and state offices. May include hiking, backpacking, canoeing, horseback riding. Contact above number to locate state offices

Sierra Club Outings
730 Polk St.
San Francisco, CA 94109
(415) 923-5630
Offers tours of different lengths for all ages throughout the United States. Outings may include backpacking, hiking, biking, skiing, and water excursions

Smithsonian Study Tours and Seminars
1100 Jefferson Dr. SW
MRC 702
Washington, D.C. 20560
(202) 357-4700
Offers extended tours, cruises, research expeditions, and seminars throughout the United States

REGIONAL

Arizona Office of Tourism
1100 W. Washington St.
Phoenix, AZ 85007
(602) 542-8687
Assists in travel and accommodation planning. Provides information on most major private tour operators within the state, including Colorado River and Grand Canyon canoe and raft guides

Arizona State Parks
1300 W. Washington St.
Phoenix, AZ 85007
(602) 542-4174
Central visitor center for state's public lands and parks. Furnishes specific information on parks, including hours, tours, camping, and fishing

The Navajo Nation
Tourism Office
P.O. Box 9000
Window Rock, AZ 86515
(520) 871-6647
Regulates travelers within Navajo lands. Distributes backcountry, camping, and horse-guided tour permits. Furnishes information on Navajo lands within national and state parks

New Mexico Department of Parks and Recreation
Villagra Building
P.O. Box 1147
Santa Fe, NM 87504
(505) 827-7465
Furnishes information on camping, trails, and travel in all state parks

New Mexico Department of Tourism
P.O. Box 20003
Santa Fe, NM 87503
(505) 827-7400
Furnishes travel information and state Chambers of Commerce locations as well as selection of private tour operators

How to Use This Site Guide

The following site information guide will assist you in planning your tour of the natural areas of the Southwest. Sites set in **boldface** and followed by the symbol ❖ in the text are here organized alphabetically by state. Each of the main entries is followed by the mailing address (sometimes different from the street address) and phone number of the immediate managing office, plus brief notes and a list of facilities and activities available. (A key appears on each page.)

Information on hours of operation, seasonal closings, and fees is not listed, as these vary from season to season and year to year. Please also bear in mind that responsibility for the management of some sites may change. Call well in advance to obtain maps, brochures, and pertinent, up-to-date information that will help you plan your southwestern adventures.

Each site entry in the guide includes the address and phone number of its immediate managing agency. Many of these sites are under the stewardship of a forest or park ranger or supervised from a small nearby office. Hence, in many cases, those sites will be difficult to contact directly, and it is preferable to call the managing agency.

The following umbrella organizations can provide general information for individual natural sites, as well as the area as a whole:

NEW MEXICO
Bureau of Land Management
PO 27115
Santa Fe, NM 87502
(505) 438-7400

The Nature Conservancy
New Mexico Field Office
212 East Marcy, Ste. 200
Santa Fe, NM 87501
(505) 988-3867

New Mexico Department of Game and Fish
PO 25112
Santa Fe, NM 87504
(505) 827-7911

New Mexico State Parks and Recreation
Villagra Building
PO 1147
Santa Fe, NM 87504
(505) 827-7465

New Mexico State Tourism Division
491 Old Santa Fe Trail
Santa Fe, NM 87503
(505) 827-7400
(800) 545-2040

U. S. Forest Service
517 Gold Ave. SW
Albuquerque, NM 87102
(505) 842-3292

ARIZONA
Arizona Game and Fish Department
2222 West Greenway Rd.
Phoenix, AZ 85023
(602) 942-3000

Arizona Office of Tourism
1100 West Washington
Phoenix, AZ 85007
(602) 542-8687

Arizona State Parks
1300 West Washington
Phoenix, AZ 85007
(602) 542-4174

The Nature Conservancy
Arizona Field Office
300 East University
Blvd., Ste. 230
Tucson, AZ 85705
(520) 622-3861

The Navajo Nation
Tourism Office
PO 9000
Window Rock, AZ 86515
(520) 871-6647

New Mexico

AGUIRRE SPRINGS RECREATION AREA
Bureau of Land Management
Mimbres Research Area, 1800 Marquess
Las Cruces, NM 88005
(505) 525-4300
BW, BT, C, H, MT, PA, RC, T

BANDELIER NATIONAL MONUMENT
National Park Service
HCR 1, PO 1, Suite 15
Los Alamos, NM 87544
(505) 672-3861
Accessible by foot or horseback only;
includes Frijoles Canyon
BW, C, GS, H, HR, I, MT, PA, RA, T, TG

BISTI WILDERNESS
Bureau of Land Management
1235 La Plata Highway
Farmington, NM 87401
(505) 599-8900
No mechanized equipment; collecting
prohibited; wood fires prohibited; portions of area may be closed seasonally;
primitive camping   **C, H, HR**

BITTER LAKE NATIONAL WILDLIFE REFUGE
U.S. Fish and Wildlife Service
PO 7, Roswell, NM 88202
(505) 622-6755
Includes Pecos River, Salt Creek
Wilderness Area **BT, BW, H, I, L, PA, T**

BOSQUE DEL APACHE NATIONAL WILDLIFE REFUGE
U.S. Fish and Wildlife Service, PO 1246
Socorro, NM 87801
(505) 835-1828 **BW, F, GS, H, I, MT, T**

BOTTOMLESS LAKES STATE PARK
New Mexico State Parks and Recreation
PO 1147, Santa Fe, NM 87504
(505) 624-6058
Includes seven sinkhole lakes
**BT, BW, C, CK, F, GS,
H, I, MT, PA, RA, S, T**

CAPULIN VOLCANO NATIONAL MONUMENT
National Park Service, Southwest Region
PO 728, Santa Fe, NM 87504
(505) 278-2201
Backcountry hiking prohibited; includes
Crater Rim Trail, Crater Vent Trail
BW, H, I, MT, PA, RA, T

CARLSBAD CAVERNS NATIONAL PARK
National Park Service
3225 National Parks Highway
Carlsbad, NM 88220
(505) 785-2232
Primitive camping; permit required for
campers; includes Slaughter Canyon
Cave, Goat Cave
BW, C, GS, H, I, PA, RA, T, TG

CARSON NATIONAL FOREST
U.S. Forest Service, Carson National Forest
PO 558, Taos, NM 87571
(505) 758-6200
No mechanized equipment in wilderness
areas; includes Wheeler Peak Wilderness,
Bull-of-the-Woods Meadow, Latir Peak
Wilderness, Cabresto Lake Campsite,
Echo Amphitheater, Pecos Wilderness
**BT, BW, C, CK, DS, F, H, HR, I,
L, MT, PA, RA, RC, S, T, TG, XC**

CHACO CULTURE NATIONAL HISTORICAL PARK
National Park Service, Southwest Region
PO 728
Santa Fe, NM 87504
(505) 786-7014
Wet weather makes summer travel diffi-
cult; backcountry camping not permitted;
includes Pueblo Bonito, Chaco Canyon
**BT, BW, C, GS, H, I,
MT, PA, RA, T, TG, XC**

CHAMA RIVER CANYON WILDERNESS
U.S. Forest Service, Coyote Ranger District
PO 160, Coyote, NM 87012
(505) 638-5526
No mechanized equipment in wilderness
areas; primitive camping; roads may be
impassable in wet weather; information
center at Ghost Ranch Living Museum
BW, C, CK, F, GS, H, HR, I, S

CIBOLA NATIONAL FOREST
U.S. Forest Service, Cibola National Forest
2113 Osuna NE, Suite A
Albuquerque, NM 87113
(505) 761-4650
Includes Zuni Mountains, Mount Taylor,
San Mateo Mountains, Sandia Mountain
Wilderness, Manzano Mountains,
Apache Kid Wilderness, Withington
Wilderness, Magdalena Mountains
**BT, BW, C, DS, F, H, HR, I,
MT, PA, RA, RC, T, TG, XC**

BT	Bike Trails	**CK**	Canoeing, Kayaking	**F**	Fishing	**HR**	Horseback Riding
BW	Bird-watching			**GS**	Gift Shop		
C	Camping	**DS**	Downhill Skiing	**H**	Hiking	**I**	Information Center

CIMARRON CANYON STATE PARK
New Mexico State Parks and Recreation
PO 1147, Ute Park, NM 87749
(505) 377-6271

At least one member of all camping parties must have a valid New Mexico hunting and fishing license; rock climbers need permit **BW, C, F, H, HR, MT, PA, RC, T, TG, XC**

CITY OF ROCKS STATE PARK
New Mexico State Parks and Recreation
PO 54, Faywood, NM 88034
(505) 536-2800

BW, C, H, I, PA, RA, RC, T, TG

CLAYTON LAKE STATE PARK
New Mexico State Parks and Recreation
RR 20, Seneca, NM 88437
(505) 374-8808

Includes Rock Garden, Dinosaur Trackway **BW, C, CK, F, H, I, L, MT, PA, RA, S, T, TG**

COCHITI LAKE
U.S. Army Corps of Engineers
PO 1580, Albuquerque, NM 87103
(505) 242-8302

Includes Tent Rocks **BW, C, CK, F, H, I, MT, PA, RA, S, T, TG**

COLIN NEBLETT WILDLIFE AREA
New Mexico Department
of Game and Fish
PO 1145, Raton, NM 87740
(505) 445-2311

At least one member of all camping parties must have a valid New Mexico hunting and fishing license; includes Touch-Me-Not Mountain and Palisades Sill **BW, C, F, H, HR, I, L, MT, PA, RA, RC, T, XC**

COOKES PEAK
Bureau of Land Management
Mimbres Research Area, 1800 Marquess
Las Cruces, NM 88005
(505) 525-4300

No off-road driving; primitive camping; includes Fort Cummings, Pony Hills, Massacre Peak **BW, C, H, RA, TG**

CORONADO NATIONAL FOREST
U.S. Forest Service
300 West Congress
Tucson, AZ 85701

(New Mexico portion is part of the Douglas Ranger District)
(520) 364-3468

Flash flooding occurs; bring water; no off-road driving; primitive camping **BW, C, H, MT**

DE-NA-ZIN WILDERNESS
Bureau of Land Management
1235 La Plata Highway
Farmington, NM 87401
(505) 599-8900

No mechanized equipment in wilderness areas; collecting prohibited; wood fires prohibited; portions of area may be closed seasonally; primitive camping **C, H, HR**

DRIPPING SPRINGS NATURAL AREA
Bureau of Land Management
Mimbres Research Area, 1800 Marquess
Las Cruces, NM 88005
(505) 525-4300

No off-road driving; includes A. B. Cox Visitor Center, La Cueva Picnic Area **BW, GS, H, I, MT, PA, RA, RC, TG**

EDWARD SARGENT FISH AND WILDLIFE MANAGEMENT AREA
New Mexico Department
of Game and Fish
Villagra Building, PO 25112
Santa Fe, NM 87504
(505) 827-7882

Seasonal; no motorized vehicles permitted; camping in designated areas only **BW, C, F, H, HR, XC**

EL MALPAIS NATIONAL CONSERVATION AREA
Bureau of Land Management
PO 846, Grants, NM 87020
(505) 287-7911

Primitive camping; includes La Ventana Natural Arch, The Narrows **BW, BT, C, GS, H, I, MT, PA, RA, T, TG, XC**

EL MALPAIS NATIONAL MONUMENT
National Park Service
PO 939, Grants, NM 87020
(505) 287-3407

Primitive camping; permit required for backcountry campers; includes Sandstone Bluffs Overlook, Zuni-Acoma Trail, El Calderon, Big Tubes **BW, C, GS, H, I, MT, PA, RA**

L Lodging	**PA** Picnic Areas	**RC** Rock Climbing	**TG** Tours, Guides
MT Marked Trails	**RA** Ranger-led Activities	**S** Swimming	**XC** Cross-country Skiing
		T Toilets	

EL MORRO NATIONAL MONUMENT
National Park Service, Route 2, PO 43
Ramah, NM 87321
(505) 783-4226
Includes Inscription Rock
BW, C, GS, H, I, MT, PA, RA, T

FLORIDA MOUNTAINS
Bureau of Land Management
Mimbres Research Area, 1800 Marquess
Las Cruces, NM 88005
(505) 525-4300
No off-road driving; primitive camping
BW, C, H, PA, RC

GHOST RANCH LIVING MUSEUM
U.S. Forest Service, Carson National Forest
PO 558, Taos, NM 87571
(505) 685-4312
**BT, BW, C, CK, F, GS, H, HR, I,
MT, PA, RA, RC, S, T, TG, XC**

**GILA CLIFF DWELLINGS NATIONAL
MONUMENT**
U.S. Forest Service, Route 11, PO 100
Silver City, NM 88061
(505) 536-9461
BW, C, CK, F, GS, H, I, MT, RA, T, TG

GILA NATIONAL FOREST
U.S. Forest Service
Forest Supervisor's Office
3005 East Camino Del Bosque
Silver City, NM 88061
(505) 388-8201
Includes Gila Wilderness, Aldo Leopold
Wilderness, Blue Range Wilderness,
Mangas Springs, Lightfoot Hot Springs,
Catwalk, Cherry Creek Campground,
Pueblo Park Campground, Lake Roberts,
Lake Quemado, Lake Snow
**BW, C, CK, DS, F, GS, H, HR,
I, L, MT, PA, RA, RC, S, T, XC**

GUADALUPE CANYON
Bureau of Land Management
1800 Marquess, Las Cruces, NM 88005
(505) 525-4300   **BW, C, H**

HERON LAKE STATE PARK
New Mexico State Parks and Recreation
PO 6458 ,Navajo, NM 87419
(505) 588-7470
Includes Rio Chama Trail Head
**BT, BW, C, CK, F, H,
I, MT, PA, RA, S, T, XC**

ICE CAVES
12000 Ice Caves Road
Grants, NM 87020
(505) 783-4303
Includes Bandera Volcano   **H, MT, PA, T**

KIOWA NATIONAL GRASSLANDS
U.S. Forest Service, Cibola National Forest
16 North 2nd Street
Clayton, NM 88415
(505) 374-9652   **BW, C, F, H, I, L, RC, T**

LINCOLN NATIONAL FOREST
U.S. Forest Service
1101 New York Avenue
Alamogordo, NM 88310
(505) 434-7200
Includes Sacramento Mountains, Sierra
Blanca, White Mountain Wilderness,
Capitan Mountain Wilderness, Guadalupe
Mountains, Sunspot Solar Observatory,
Apache Point Stellar Observatory
**BT, BW, C, DS, F, GS, H, HR,
I, MT, PA, RA, RC, S, T, TG, XC**

LOWER BOX
Bureau of Land Management
Mimbres Research Area, 1800 Marquess
Las Cruces, NM 88005
(505) 525-4300
No off-road driving; primitive camping
BW, C, CK, F, H, MT, S

MAXWELL NATIONAL WILDLIFE REFUGE
U.S. Fish and Wildlife Service
PO 276, Maxwell, NM 87728
(505) 375-2331
Camping is primitive and seasonal; geese
plentiful November–February; includes
Lakes Twelve, Thirteen, and Fourteen
BW, C, CK, F, I, PA, T

MESCALERO SAND DUNES
Bureau of Land Management
PO 1857, Roswell, NM 88202
(505) 624-1790
Primitive camping; includes Mescalero
Sands Outstanding Natural Area, Fort
Stanton Caves, Torgac'x Caves
BW, C, H, HR, PA, RA, T, TG

MORGAN LAKE
U.S. Fish and Wildlife Service
PO 1480, Window Rock, AZ 86515
(520) 645-6451
Fish not edible   **CK, F, PA, T**

BT	Bike Trails	**CK**	Canoeing, Kayaking	**F**	Fishing	**HR**	Horseback Riding
BW	Bird-watching			**GS**	Gift Shop		
C	Camping	**DS**	Downhill Skiing	**H**	Hiking	**I**	Information Center

NARBONA PASS
New Mexico State Parks and Recreation
Navajo Nation Tourism Office
PO 9000
Window Rock, AZ 86515
(520) 871-6647
Also known as Washington Pass **C, PA**

NEW MEXICO GAME AND FISH PRAIRIE CHICKEN AREAS
Bureau of Land Management
PO 1857, Roswell, NM 88202
(505) 624-1790
April is peak month; primitive camping
BW, C, H, PA, T, TG

NORTH DUNE OFF-ROAD VEHICLE RECREATION AREA
Bureau of Land Management
PO 1857, Roswell, NM 88202
(505) 624-1790
Primitive camping; 4WD recommended
BW, C, H, HR, PA, RA, T, TG

ORGAN MOUNTAINS
Bureau of Land Management
Mimbres Research Area
1800 Marquess
Las Cruces, NM 88005
(505) 525-4300
No off-road driving; primitive camping;
includes Baylor Pass, Pine Tree Trail
BT, BW, C, H, HR, MT, PA, RC

ORILLA VERDE RECREATION AREA
Bureau of Land Management
Taos Resource Area
224 Cruz Alta Road, Taos, NM 87571
(505) 758-8851
BW, C, CK, F, GS, H, HR, I, L, MT, PA, RA, S, T, TG

PECOS WILDERNESS
Pecos Ranger District
PO Drawer 3
Pecos, NM 87552
(505) 757-6121
BW, C, F, H, HR, MT, RC, XC

PRESILLA WILDERNESS STUDY AREA
Bureau of Land Management
198 Neel Avenue
Socorro, NM 87801
(505) 835-0412
Primitive camping; includes Arroyo del
Tajo Canyon **BW, C, H, MT, RA, TG**

RATTLESNAKE SPRINGS
National Park Service
3225 National Parks Highway
Carlsbad, NM 88220
(505) 885-8884 **BW, H, MT, PA, RA, T, TG**

RIO CHAMA WILDLIFE AND FISHING AREA
New Mexico Department of Game and Fish
Villagra Building,
PO 25112
Santa Fe, NM 87504
(505) 827-7882
Camping in designated areas only; in-
cludes Chama River; call (505) 758-8851
for BLM-managed Wild and Scenic River
BW, C, F, H, HR, XC

RIO GRANDE NATURE CENTER STATE PARK
New Mexico State Parks and Recreation
PO 1147,
Santa Fe, NM 87504
(505) 344-7240
No picnicking or pets; includes Four
Acre Wetland, Visitor Center
BW, GS, H, I, MT, RA, T, TG

RIO GRANDE WILD AND SCENIC RIVER
Bureau of Land Management
Taos Resource Area,
224 Cruz Alta Road
Taos, NM 87571
(505) 758-8851
Boating permits necessary in summer;
includes Visitor Center, Rio Grande High
Bridge, Black Rock Spring
BT, BW, C, CK, F, GS, H, I, L, MT, PA, RA, T, TG, XC

ROCK HOUND STATE PARK
New Mexico State Parks and Recreation
PO 1064, Deming,
NM 88030
(505) 546-6182
BW, C, H, I, MT, PA, RA, RC, T, TG

SANDIA MOUNTAINS
U.S. Forest Service
Cibola National Forest,
Sandia Ranger District
11776 Highway 337, Tijeras, NM 87059
(505) 281-3304
Includes La Luz Trail, Crest Spur Trail,
Crest Trail, Tijeras Pueblo, Sandia Cave
BT, BW, C, DS, GS, H, HR, I, L, MT, PA, RA, RC, T, TG, XC

L	Lodging	PA	Picnic Areas	RC	Rock Climbing	TG	Tours, Guides
MT	Marked Trails	RA	Ranger-led Activities	S	Swimming	XC	Cross-country Skiing
				T	Toilets		

Site Guide

SAN PEDRO PARKS WILDERNESS
Cuba Ranger District, PO 130
Cuba, NM 87013, (505) 289-3264
  Primitive camping
BW, C, H, HR, MT, XC

SANTA FE NATIONAL FOREST
U.S. Forest Service
PO 1689, Santa Fe, NM 87504
(505) 988-6940
  Includes Chama River Canyon
  Wilderness, Pecos Wilderness, Sangre de
  Cristo Mountains, Jemez Mountains, San
  Pedro Parks Wilderness, Dome
  Wilderness; 4WD recommended
**BT, BW, C, CK, DS, F, GS, H, HR,
I, MT, PA, RA, RC, S, T, TG, XC**

SHIPROCK
New Mexico State Parks and Recreation
Navajo Nation Tourism Office
PO 9000, Window Rock, AZ 86515
(520) 871-6647   **BW, GS, HR, I, PA, TG**

SITTING BULL FALLS
U.S. Forest Service
Federal Building Room 159
Carlsbad, NM 88220
(505) 885-4181   **BW, H, MT, PA, S, T**

SNAKE BRIDGE
Navajo Nation/Tourism Office
PO 9000, Window Rock, AZ 86515
(520) 871-6647
  Permission required at Sanostee Trading
  Post; not a tourist area

STONE LAKE
Jicarilla Apache Tribe
PO 507, Duke, NM 87528
(505) 759-3242
  Primitive camping **BW, C, CK, F, H, T, XC**

TAJIQUE CANYON
U.S. Forest Service
Mountainair Ranger District
PO 69, Mountainair, NM 87036
(505) 847-2990
BT, BW, C, H, HR, MT, PA, T, TG, XC

TENT ROCKS
Bureau of Land Management
435 Montano NE, Albuquerque, NM 87107
(505) 761-8700
  No mechanized equipment
BW, H, I, M, RA, TG

VALLEY OF FIRES RECREATION AREA
Bureau of Land Management
PO 1857, Roswell, NM 88202
(505) 624-1790
BW, C, GS, H, I, L, MT, PA, RA, T, TG

VOLCANO PARK
Open Space Division
PO 1293, Albuquerque, NM 87103
(505) 873-6620
  Includes Vulcan Volcano, Bond Volcano
BW, H, HR, MT

WHISKEY LAKE
U.S. Fish and Wildlife Service
PO 1480, Window Rock, AZ 86515
(520) 871-6451
  Seasonal   **BW, CK, F, H, T**

WHITE SANDS NATIONAL MONUMENT
National Park Service, PO 1086
Holloman Air Force Base, NM 88330
(505) 479-6124
  Closes for military activities; primitive
  camping; includes Dunes Drive
C, GS, H, I, MT, PA, RA, T, TG

ARIZONA

ALAMO LAKE STATE PARK
Arizona State Parks
1300 West Washington
Phoenix, AZ 85007
(602) 542-4174
  Remote desert area
BW, C, F, H, PA, T

APACHE-SITGREAVES NATIONAL FOREST
Forest Supervisor's Office
PO 640
Springerville,AZ 85938
(520) 333-4301
  Reservations recommended at camp-
  ground; Mount Baldy Peak is off limits;
  includes Mount Baldy Wilderness,
  Crescent Lake, Big Lake, Mogollon Rim,
  Coronado Scenic Highway, Greer Lake
  Recreation Area, Fool Hollow Lake
**BT, BW, C, CK, F, H,
HR, I, MT, PA, RA, RC, S, T, TG, XC**

ARAVAIPA CANYON WILDERNESS AREA
Bureau of Land Management
Safford District Office
711 14th Avenue,
Safford, AZ 85546
(520) 428-4040

BT Bike Trails	**CK** Canoeing, Kayaking	**F** Fishing	**HR** Horseback Riding
BW Bird-watching	**DS** Downhill Skiing	**GS** Gift Shop	**I** Information Center
C Camping		**H** Hiking	

Access limited; permit required; no mechanized equipment; primitive camping only; maximum stay 3 days/2 nights
BW, C, H, HR, I, S, T, TG

ARIZONA-SONORA DESERT MUSEUM
2021 North Kinney Road
Tucson, AZ 85743
(520) 883-2702 (machine)
BT, BW, GS, H, I, MT, RA, T

ARRASTRA MOUNTAIN WILDERNESS AREA
Bureau of Land Management
Lower Gila Resource Area
2015 West Deer Valley Road
Phoenix, AZ 85027
(602) 780-8090
Includes People's Canyon; no bicycles or motorized vehicles **BW, C, H, HR, RC**

BABOQUIVARI PEAK WILDERNESS
Bureau of Land Management
Tucson Resource Area
12661 East Broadway Blvd.
Tucson, AZ 85748
(520) 722-4289
Advanced climbing techniques are required to reach summit of Baboquivari Peak; primitive camping only; access by foot only; private lands may block access to trailheads **BW, C, H, RC**

BILL WILLIAMS RIVER
NATIONAL WILDLIFE REFUGE
U.S. Fish and Wildlife Service
60911 Highway 95
Parker, AZ 85344
(520) 667-4144
No mechanized vehicles **BW, F, H**

BLUE RANGE PRIMITIVE AREA
U.S. Forest Service, Alpine Ranger District
PO 469 Alpine, AZ 89520
(520) 339-4384
Remote; river dries up in early summer; be aware of red flag warnings (no campfires) **BT, BW, C, F, GS, H, I, MT, PA, RC, T, TG**

BOYCE THOMPSON SOUTHWESTERN ARBORETUM
37615 East Highway 60
Superior, AZ 85273
(520) 689-2811, -2723
Day use only
BW, GS, H, I, MT, PA, RA, T, TG

BUENOS AIRES
NATIONAL WILDLIFE REFUGE
U.S. Fish and Wildlife Service
PO 109 Sasabe, AZ 85633
(520) 823-4251
Primitive camping
BT, BW, C, H, HR, I, MT, RA, T, TG

CABEZA PRIETA
NATIONAL WILDLIFE REFUGE
U.S. Fish and Wildlife Service
1611 North 2nd Avenue, Ajo, AZ 85321
(520) 387-6483
Access limited and by permit only; 4WD required **BW, C, H, I**

CACTUS PLAIN
Bureau of Land Management
Havasu Resource Area
3189 Sweetwater Avenue
Lake Havasu, AZ 86406
(520) 855-8017
Limited motorized vehicle access; primitive camping only **BW, C, H, HR**

CANELO HILLS CIENEGA PRESERVE
The Nature Conservancy
PO 815,
Patagonia, AZ 85624
(520) 394-2400
Extremely fragile area; please make prior arrangements with preserve manager
BW, H, I, MT, T, TG

CANYON DE CHELLY
NATIONAL MONUMENT
National Park Service
PO 588,
Chinle, AZ 86503
(520) 674-5500
Park ranger or Navajo guide must accompany visitors; arrangements made at visitor center; includes Canyon del Muerto, Monument Canyon, Black Rock Canyon, White House Ruin
BW, C, GS, H, HR, I, L, PA, RA, T, TG

CATHEDRAL ROCK
U.S. Forest Service, Sedona Ranger District
PO 300,
Sedona, AZ 86339
(520) 282-4119
Call ranger station for directions; primitive camping; includes Red Rock Crossing–Crescent Moon Day Use Area
BW, C, F, H, I, MT, PA, S, T

L	Lodging	**PA**	Picnic Areas	**RC**	Rock Climbing	**TG** Tours, Guides
MT	Marked Trails	**RA**	Ranger-led Activities	**S**	Swimming	**XC** Cross-country Skiing
				T	Toilets	

CAVE CREEK CANYON
U.S. Forest Service, Douglas Ranger District
RR 1, PO 228 R, Douglas, AZ 85607
(520) 364-3468
> Flash floods July–August, November–
> February; bring water; includes Cathedral
> Rock, Silver Peak, Skull Eyes, Rustler Park
> Campground, Southwestern Research
> Station **BT, BW, C, GS, H, I, L,
> MT, PA, RA, RC, T, TG, XC**

CHIRICAHUA NATIONAL MONUMENT
National Park Service
Dos Cabezas Route, PO 6500
Willcox, AZ 85643
(520) 824-3560
> Be wary of lightning during summer
> months; no backcountry camping; in-
> cludes Pinnacles and Balance Rocks,
> Faraway Ranch
> **BW, C, GS, H, HR, I, MT, PA, RA, T, TG**

CIBOLA NATIONAL WILDLIFE REFUGE
U.S. Fish and Wildlife Service
PO AP, Blythe, CA 92226
(520) 857-3253
> Includes Cibola Lake (open March
> 15–Labor Day), Goose Loop (open
> November–February)
> **BW, CK, F, I, RA, T, TG**

COCONINO NATIONAL FOREST
U.S. Forest Service
2323 East Greenlaw Lane
Flagstaff, AZ 86004
(520) 527-3600
> Most campgrounds open summer only,
> 14-day stay limit; includes Bell Trail,
> Mormon Lake, Stoneman Lake, Rim Road,
> Kehl Springs Campground, Kachina Peak
> Wilderness, Red Rock Secret Mountain
> Wilderness, Wet Beaver Creek Wilderness,
> Oak Creek Canyon Recreation Area
> **BT, BW, C, CK, DS, F, GS, H,
> HR, I, MT, PA, S, T, TG, XC**

CORONADO NATIONAL FOREST
U.S. Forest Service
300 West Congress,
Tucson, AZ 85701
(520) 670-4552
> Includes Crystal Cave, Sabino Canyon,
> Pusch River Wilderness, Mount Lemmon,
> Pajarita Wilderness, Sycamore Canyon
> **BT, BW, C, DS, GS, H, HR,
> I, L, MT, PA, RA, RC, T, TG**

DEAD HORSE RANCH STATE PARK
PO 144, Cottonwood, AZ 86326
(520) 634-5283
> **BW, C, F, H, I, MT, PA, T**

DRAGOON MOUNTAINS
U.S. Forest Service
Douglas Ranger District
RR 1, PO 228 R, Douglas, AZ 85607
(520) 364-3468
> Flash floods July–August, November–
> February; includes Little Dragoon
> Mountains, East Cochise Stronghold,
> Mount Glenn
> **BT, BW, C, H, HR, I, MT, PA, RC, T, TG**

EMPIRE CIENEGA RESOURCE CONSERVATION AREA
Bureau of Land Management
Tucson Resource Area, 12661 East Broadway
Tucson, AZ 85748
(520) 722-4289
> No water or parking, primitive camping
> only **BT, BW, C, H, HR, PA**

FORT APACHE INDIAN RESERVATION
Fort Apache Culture Center
PO 507, Fort Apache, AZ 85926
(520) 338-4625
> Permits for camping, fishing, boating,
> etc. available at the White Mountain
> Recreation Enterprise; includes Sunrise
> Lake, Sunrise Ski Resort, Hawley Lake
> **BT, BW, C, CK, DS, F, GS, H,
> I, L, MT, PA, RC, S, T, XC**

GLEN CANYON NATIONAL RECREATION AREA
National Park Service
PO 1507, Page, AZ 86040
(520) 645-8404
> Permit required for boaters bringing their
> own boat; includes Rainbow Bridge
> **C, CK, F, GS, H, I, L, PA, RA, S, T, TG**

GRAND CANYON NATIONAL PARK
National Park Service Trip Planner
PO 129, Grand Canyon, AZ 86023
(520) 638-7888
> Be prepared for crowds during spring,
> summer, and early fall; backpackers in-
> terested in overnight excursions must
> write at least 6 months in advance; in-
> cludes South Rim, Cedar Ridge
> **BW, C, CK, F, GS, H, I, L,
> MT, PA, RA, T, TG, XC**

BT	Bike Trails	**CK**	Canoeing, Kayaking	**F**	Fishing	**HR**	Horseback Riding
BW	Bird-watching	**DS**	Downhill Skiing	**GS**	Gift Shop	**I**	Information Center
C	Camping			**H**	Hiking		

HAVASU NATIONAL WILDLIFE REFUGE
U.S. Fish and Wildlife Service
PO 3009, Needles, CA 92363
(619) 326-3853
Includes Topock Marsh, Lake Havasu,
Topock Gorge; gorge accessible by boat
and foot only   **BW, C, CK, F, H, S, TG**

HUALAPAI MOUNTAIN PARK
Mohave City Park
PO 7000, Kingman, AZ 86402
(520) 757-3859
Public-use cabins; includes Aspen Peak
Trail, Hayden Peak Trail.
**BT, BW, C, H, HR, I, L,
MT, PA, RA, RC, T, TG, XC**

IMPERIAL NATIONAL WILDLIFE REFUGE
U.S. Fish and Wildlife Service
PO 1306, Albuquerque, NM 87103
(520) 783-3371
Includes Painted Desert Trail, Red Cloud
Mine Road
BW, CK, F, GS, H, I, PA, RA, S, T, TG

KAIBAB NATIONAL FOREST
U.S. Forest Service
Williams Ranger District
200 Railroad Avenue
Williams, AZ 86046
(520) 635-4061
All campers must be $^1/_4$ mile from roads
and water sources; includes Kanab Creek
Wilderness   **BT, BW, C, CK, DS, F, GS,
H, HR, I, L, MT, PA, RA, T, TG, XC**

KARTCHNER CAVERNS STATE PARK
Arizona State Parks
1300 West Washington
Phoenix, AZ 85007
(602) 542-4174
Call in advance; includes Whetstone
Mountains
BW, C, GS, H, I, MT, PA, RA, T, TG

KOFA NATIONAL WILDLIFE REFUGE
U.S. Fish and Wildlife Service
PO 6290
Yuma, AZ 85366
(520) 783-7861
Primitive camping only; includes Palm
Canyon and Castle Dome Range
BW, C, H, HR

LAKE MEAD
NATIONAL RECREATION AREA
National Park Service

601 Nevada Highway
Boulder City, NV 89005
(702) 293-8907
Includes Rogers and Bluepoint Springs,
Redstone Area, Black Canyon,
Grapevine Canyon Petroglyphs
**BT, BW, C, CK, F, GS, H, I,
L, MT, PA, RA, S, T, TG**

LOST DUTCHMAN STATE PARK
Arizona State Parks, 6109 North Apache Trail
Apache Junction, AZ 85219
(602) 982-4485
Access to Superstition Wilderness via
Apache Trail; primitive camping
BT, BW, C, H, I, MT, PA, RA, T, TG

MADERA CANYON
U.S. Forest Service
Nogales Ranger District
2251 North Grand Avenue
Nogales, AZ 85621
(520) 281-2296
Access limited; primitive camping pro-
hibited
BT, BW, C, GS, H, I, L, MT, PA, T, TG

MITTRY LAKE WILDLIFE AREA
Arizona Game and Fish Department
9140 East County 10½ Street
Yuma, AZ 85365
(520) 342-0091
Roads are not well marked; primitive
camping only; includes Betty's Kitchen
Interpretive Area
BW, C, CK, F, H, PA, RA, T, TG

MONUMENT VALLEY NATIONAL
MONUMENT
Monument Valley Navajo Tribal Park
PO 93,
Monument Valley, UT 84536
(801) 727-3287
No backcountry camping; visitors can
arrange for guided tour through monu-
ment, or pay fee; includes Mystery
Valley   **BW, C, H, I, RA, TG**

MOUNT TRUMBULL
Bureau of Land Management
Arizona Strip District
Vermilion Resource Area
390 North 3050 East, St. George, UT 84770
(801) 673-3545
Only accessible during dry season; primi-
tive camping; no amenities   **C, TG**

L	Lodging	**PA**	Picnic Areas	**RC**	Rock Climbing	**TG**	Tours, Guides
MT	Marked Trails	**RA**	Ranger-led Activities	**S**	Swimming	**XC**	Cross-country Skiing
				T	Toilets		

273

Museum of Northern Arizona
Route 4,
PO 720
Flagstaff, AZ 86001
(520) 774-5211   **GS, I, MT, T, TG**

Organ Pipe Cactus National Monument
National Park Service
Rte. 1, PO 100, Ajo, AZ 85321
(602) 387-6849
Bring water; includes Quitobaquito
Springs, Ajo Mountains
BW, C, GS, H, I, MT, PA, RA, T

Paria Canyon–Vermilion Cliffs Wilderness
Bureau of Land Management
Kanab Resource Area
318 North 1st East
Kanab, UT 84741
(801) 644-2672
Most of area not accessible by vehicle,
no mechanized transport   **BW, C, H, T**

Patagonia–Sonoita Creek Preserve
The Nature Conservancy
PO 815
Patagonia, AZ 85624
(520) 394-2400
No picnicking; groups are advised to
call ahead to make arrangements for
guides   **BW, H, I, MT, RA, T, TG**

Petrified Forest National Park
National Park Service
PO 2217
Petrified Forest NP, AZ 86028
(520) 524-6228
Weather is mercurial; permit required
for overnight campers, primitive camp-
ing; includes Painted Desert Wilderness,
Kachina Point, Chinle Point, Puerco
Ruin, Newspaper Rock, Blue Mesa,
Agate Bridge, Jasper Forest, Crystal
Forest, Long Logs Trail, Rainbow Forest
C, GS, H, I, PA, RA, T

Prescott National Forest
U.S. Forest Service
344 South Cortez
Prescott, AZ 86303
(520) 771-4700
Includes Castle Creek Wilderness,
Hassayampa Lake, Mount Union, Granite
Mountain Wilderness, Thumb Butte
BT, BW, C, CK, F, GS, H, HR, I, MT, PA, RC, T, TG

Ramsey Canyon Preserve
The Nature Conservancy
27 Ramsey Canyon Road
Hereford, AZ 85615
(520) 378-2785
Hiking permit necessary; reservations
necessary for public-use cabins
BW, GS, H, I, L, MT, RA, T, TG

Saguaro National Monument
National Park Service
3693 South Old Spanish Trail
Tucson, AZ 85730
(520) 670-6680
Permit required for backcountry camping
BT, BW, C, GS, H, I, MT, PA, RA, T, TG

Salt River Canyon
U.S. Forest Service
Globe Ranger District
Rte 1, PO 33, Globe, AZ 85501
(520) 425-7189
Kayakers and car drivers need permission
from Fort Apache Indian Reservation; river
is vigorous whitewater; primitive camping
BW, C, CK, F, H, T, TG

San Pedro Riparian National Conservation Area
Bureau of Land Management
1763 Paseo San Luis,
Sierra Vista, AZ 85635
(520) 458-3559
Primitive camping only; permit required
for overnight camping; no mechanized
vehicles   **BW, C, GS, H, HR, I, MT, PA, RA, S, T, TG**

Slide Rock State Park
PO 10358,
Sedona, AZ 86336
(520) 282-3034
No glass containers or pets
BW, F, I, MT, PA, S, T, TG

Sycamore Canyon Wilderness
U.S. Forest Service
Sedona Ranger District
PO 300, Sedona,
AZ 86336
(520) 282-4119
Primitive camping; very rugged hike;
visitors are advised to bring water; no
mechanized vehicles; includes Taylor
Cabin (cowboy artifacts)
BW, C, F, H, HR, MT, S

BT	Bike Trails	**CK**	Canoeing, Kayaking	**F**	Fishing	**HR**	Horseback Riding
BW	Bird-watching			**GS**	Gift Shop		
C	Camping	**DS**	Downhill Skiing	**H**	Hiking	**I**	Information Center

TONTO NATIONAL FOREST
U.S. Forest Service
2324 East McDowell Road
Phoenix, AZ 85006
(602) 225-5200
    Includes Tonto Natural Bridge, Mazatzal
    Wilderness, Superstition Wilderness,
    Weaver's Needle, Apache Trail, Fish
    Creek Overlook, Roosevelt Lake
                BT, BW, C, CK, F, GS, H, HR,
                I, L, MT, PA, RA, RC, S, T, TG

TONTO NATIONAL MONUMENT
HC 02, PO 4602
Roosevelt, AZ 85545
(520) 467-2241
    Desert conditions; reservations needed
    for upper ruins tour; day use only
                BW, GS, H, I, MT, PA, RA, T, TG

TOROWEAP
Grand Canyon National Park
PO 129
Grand Canyon, AZ 86023
(520) 638-7888
    Permit required for backcountry camp-
    ing; primitive camping only; road im-
    passable most of the year; bring your
    own water   **C, H**

TUCSON MOUNTAIN PARK
Pima County Parks and Recreation
1204 West Silverlake Road
Tucson, AZ 85713
(520) 740-2690
    Includes Arizona-Sonora Desert Museum
                    BT, BW, C, GS, H,
                    HR, MT, PA, RA, T, TG

TUZIGOOT NATIONAL MONUMENT
National Park Service
PO 68, Clarkdale, AZ 86324
(520) 634-5564   **GS, I, MT, T, TG**

VIRGIN RIVER CANYON
RECREATION AREA
Bureau of Land Management
225 North Bluff Street
St. George, UT 84770
(801) 673-3545   **BW, C, H, MT, PA, T**

WALNUT CANYON NATIONAL MONUMENT
National Park Service
Walnut Canyon Road
Flagstaff, AZ 86004
(520) 526-0571
    Reservations required for ranger-led
    walks; day use only; includes Island
    Trail, Rim Trail
                        I, MT, PA, RA, T, TG

WILLCOX PLAYA (GAME AND FISH UNIT)
Arizona Game and Fish Department
555 North Greasewood
Tucson, AZ 85745
(520) 628-5376
    Primitive camping only; includes Crane
    Lake, which is closed during winter
    months   **BW, C, H, MT, TG**

WILLCOX PLAYA (BLM UNIT)
Bureau of Land Management
711 14th Avenue
Safford, AZ 85546
(520) 428-4040
    Primitive camping only   **BW, C, H**

WUPATKI NATIONAL MONUMENT
National Park Service
HC 33, PO 444A
Flagstaff, AZ 86004
(520) 556-7040
    Permit required for off-trail travel; day
    use only
                BW, GS, H, I, MT, PA, RA, T, TG

L Lodging	**PA** Picnic Areas	**RC** Rock Climbing	**TG** Tours, Guides
MT Marked	**RA** Ranger-led	**S** Swimming	**XC** Cross-country
Trails	Activities	**T** Toilets	Skiing

INDEX

Numbers in **bold**
indicate illustrations;
numbers in **_bold italics_**
indicate maps.

PHOTOGRAPH CREDITS

All photography by George H. H. Huey except for the following:

Front cover: George H. H. Huey
xii: Utah State Historical Society, Salt Lake City, UT (photo #917.911)
xiv–xv: Yale Collection of Western Americana, Beinecke Rare Book and Manuscript Library, New Haven, CT
6–7: National Museum of American Art, Smithsonian Institution, Washington, D.C. (Acc. #L.1968.84.2)
12, 13: John Cancalosi, Tucson, AZ
19: Mary Clay/Tom Stack & Associates, Colorado Springs, CO
20–21: Edward S. Curtis/National Anthropological Archives, Smithsonian Institution, Washington, D.C., Photo No. 9.3 (75-11252)
26–27: Steven Sloman/Sloan Collection of American Paintings, Valparaiso University Museum of Art, Valparaiso, IN
38: John Cancalosi, Tucson, AZ
39: Thomas D. Mangelsen/Images of Nature, Jackson, WY
94, 95: Thomas Kitchin/Tom Stack & Associates
100: Ray V. Davis/By permission of Ms. Jerry F. Davis, Carlsbad, NM, from the collection of Dr. William R. Halliday, Nashville, TN
101: Merlin D. Tuttle/Bat Conservation International, Austin, TX
102–3: John Cancalosi, Tucson, AZ
111: Cornell Laboratory of Ornithology, Ithaca, NY

113, top: Arizona State Museum, University of Arizona, Tucson, AZ
113, bottom: Jerry Jacka, Phoenix, AZ
125: G. C. Kelley, Tucson, AZ
130–31: Phoenix Art Museum, AZ
138–39: John Cancalosi, Tucson, AZ
146: Milton Rand/Tom Stack & Associates
147: Thomas A. Wiewandt, Tucson, AZ
148: Library of Congress, Washington, D.C.
150: John Cancalosi, Tucson, AZ
151: G. C. Kelley, Tucson, AZ
163: E. R. Degginger/Animals Animals, Chatham, NY
168: Mark S. Thaler, Tucson, AZ
172–73, 176–77: James Tallon, Phoenix, AZ
192, L: G. C. Kelley, Tucson, AZ
195: John Cancalosi, Tucson, AZ
205: Larry Brock/Tom Stack & Associates
206: John Cancalosi, Tucson, AZ
218: Academy of Natural Sciences, Philadelphia, PA
230: Thomas A. Wiewandt/DRK Photo, Sedona, AZ
232: Thomas Moran Biographical Art Collection, East Hampton Library, East Hampton, NY
233: Cooper-Hewitt Museum of Decorative Arts and Design, Smithsonian Institution, New York, NY (Acc. #1917-17-83)
259: Library of Congress, Washington, D.C. (Photo #LC-U5Z62-7119)
Back cover: George H. H. Huey (cactus flower, owl); Milton Rand/Tom Stack & Associates (deer)

ACKNOWLEDGMENTS

The editors gratefully acknowledge the assistance of Tim Allan, Marni Davis, Jane Hoffman, Susan Kirby, and Patricia Woodruff. The following consultants also helped in the preparation of this volume: Gary M. Avey, editor and publisher of *Native Peoples* magazine, and Dallas Rhodes, Professor and Chair of Geology, Whittier College.